T0288167

THE CLAN OF THE FLAPDRAGON

AND OTHER ADVENTURES IN ETYMOLOGY

BY B. M. W. SCHRAPNEL, PH.D.

The Clan
of the Flapdragon
and Other Adventures
in Etymology

by B. M. W. Schrapnel, Ph.D.

Richard McKee

The University of Alabama Press
Tuscaloosa

The University of Alabama Press
Tuscaloosa, Alabama 35487-0380
uapress.ua.edu

These satirical essays were published originally (December 1992–
December 1996) in *OASIS, A Literary Magazine*, edited by Neal
Storrs.

Hardcover edition published 1997.
Paperback edition published 2020.
eBook edition published 2020.

Inquiries about reproducing material from this work should be
addressed to the University of Alabama Press.

Typeface: Minion Pro

Cover design: Laura L. Lineberry

Paperback ISBN: 978-0-8173-6009-2
E-ISBN: 978-0-8173-9352-6

A previous edition of this book has been cataloged by the Library of
Congress.
ISBN: 978-0-8173-0881-0 (cloth)

for Linda, Laska, and Coconut

I was raised, on the planes of Kansas
Then I was born, on the streets of L.A.
And I came of age, backstage in New Jersey
Mama don't worry, I haven't lost my way.

. . .

People change, but still the same
They gotta do what they do best
And try like this, unless I miss my guess.

from "Miss My Guess"
words and music by Harry Papagan

 CONTENTS

 PREFACE

"Yes, a regular column by Shrapnel in *Oasis* should be quite a feather in the magazine's cap."

So wrote editor/publisher Dr. Neal Storrs to my dauntless proposal of January 1993; *Oasis* had debuted in October 1992. Thus on the strength of three or four samples of writing, B. M. W. Schrapnel, Ph.D., was in on the ground level, perhaps second floor, of this fine new literary magazine out of Largo, Florida. The first installments of "Adventures in Etymology" appeared in the March 1993 issue.

My original design was to produce parodies of those columns in the popular presses by various language mavens and follow the essays with letters from disagreeing and/or irate readers, to make something like the book-length compilations of William Safire's "On Language." Schrapnel, however, was to be a bit more literary, satirical of course, and sometimes more radically environmental than his glossy rivals. In addition, the charade implied that the Adventures were appearing first in high-profile (though imaginary) publications like the *Journal of Cultural Calamity* and that magazines like *Oasis*, which could afford to buy only second serial rights, received as a consolation (or back door) prize the option to print the letters that Schrapnel's columns spawned or provoked. Each essay, then, was followed by "Cleopatra's Basket" (the letters), which for many readers is the highlight of their Schrapnel experience. By May of 1993, Dr. Storrs was receiving genuine missives containing remarks like, "The B. M. W. Schrapnel, Ph.D., piece is alone worth the price of admittance, for which my $25 check is enclosed happily."

Creative nonfiction may be the term that most properly categorizes the genre displayed here, as most of the essays contain verifiable, objective truths at their hearts. But when the adventure invariably approaches the regions of the soul, something happens. Satire storms in. Hyperbole often rains down. What began as a seemingly simple trek into the forest of language and etymology encounters a spiritual cyclone that renders the reader overpowered and boggled, like a person found near a tornado-devastated trailer park, the frazzled witness interviewed after the twister has struck and gone. Or as one letter writer analyzes from Cleopatra's Basket, "I suspect you [B. M. W. Schrapnel, Ph.D.] are a passionate man of letters who tries at times to disguise his outrage and frustration with literary peers and colleagues with satire and the less accessible forms of irony and odd wit. . . . Those 'etymologies' of yours are often springboards into darker and ignored truths. You do not fool me."

Indeed these adventures in etymology often lumber above and below anything to which the professional linguist, lexicographer, or literary critic might strive or stoop, as delving into a word's past perchance delivers one into a contemporary and historical milieu unforeseen at journey's outset. A case in point here is B. M. W. Schrapnel's review of William F. Scarlet's unauthorized biography of Robin Hood, which traces the slang usage of *hood* back to Shakespeare and reveals a plot several generations long—perpetrated by the likes of Alexander Pope and Washington Irving—to remove from literary history the Bard's original slang coinage. "Hoodunit?" is a courageous exposé that leaves both reviewer and author open to the vengeance of embarrassed descendants of Pope, Irving, and a host of sleazy lexicographers who also executed the coverup. Thus for Dr. Schrapnel, language is not merely a communication vehicle. It is a perscrutation of suspicious and chaotic worlds, a steed to carry him into regions sometimes resplendent in blinding and illuminating verities and occasionally strewn with boulders of bewilderment. So the language of Schrapnel, contrary to the nonsense often printed and spoken in the mainstream (and in some crannies of the academy), endeavors and dares to make some sense out of cloudy circumstances in a benumbed cosmos. And while you may think Schrapnel's seemingly eccentric and erratic positions—his diction and syntax too—purely outrageous and posturing, there is an eerie resonance about his words, like the distant thunder of a locomotive crashing into an army convoy stalled at the crossing.

In some ways I regard B. M. W. Schrapnel, Ph.D., as my Frankenstein (that's FRONK en steen!), not a pseudonym, but a fictional character. And much like Mary Shelley's wonderful creature amok in a fearful and selfish society, he seems to be cut off from the usual flow of critics and literary persons by the monstrousness of his style and Weltanschauung and his occasionally tacky Weltschmerz. The raw love he harbors for delightfully principled language and literature—to some an art so rare in this age of aesthetic famine—has not yet reduced him to hate and isolation, as it does so many writers afflicted with the satire syndrome. But I will leave the reader to pervert and project the rest of this analogy.

If Schrapnel, then, is a fictional character (thankfully so for many), another interpretive option opens up for the truly postmodern peruser; for we live in an age that requires us to have our options, plan B, subtext, alternative, escape route, whatever. By this I mean: *The Clan of the Flapdragon and Other Adventures in Etymology* can be read not only as creative nonfiction but also as a species of novella in letters. Schrapnel's essays are, on one level, meditations, letters to a needful readership. To these missives the readers reply, establishing a fragile yet tense narrative. I have a former colleague to thank for suggesting such a reading. She insists on anonymity and said to me one evening, after spending two days with the manuscript, "I feel like I've been harassed by a fictional character who probably wouldn't like me either."

Again, think about it. Schrapnel is the huffy and sometimes zany protagonist campaigning for the literary arts, logic, and moderately good sense and taste. It is a journey not without snares, as the book has its antagonists, those hissing from Cleopatra's Basket, who frequently represent and define the difficult task that all heroes undertake. In his quest, Schrapnel goes forth to engage the forces of stupidity and tasteless nihilism that threaten to usurp his world. Thus Elvis Peebles, the master of missive invective, if not the arch villain in the tale, is surely a breed of insidious trickster, challenging the Doctor on nearly every diagnosis and deed, as do so many others. Then there is the subplot so often present in heroic dramas. In this story we have Forrest Jones, the underground ecowarrior whose battle against those who would depredate the American environment parallels B. M. W. Schrapnel's war on the iconoclasts who batter Western culture. And it is the letter, one of the oldest and most treasured of literary forms, that establishes and maintains the conflict—the dialogue—that places *The Clan of the Flapdragon* in a long and storied genre dating back to the century of Samuel Richardson and resonating still in contemporary writers like John Barth—yes, the epistolary novel.

Well, why not?

Sobering too, perhaps, is a cognizance that the adventures are not over, that the grand undertaking must proceed until the clash between the forces of good and evil reaches a decisive closure. It is the quintessential showdown, then, and one that you must enter, or else. I could be in error here, but I do not believe I am.

Richard McKee
Cedar Key

# ACKNOWLEDGMENTS

Because "Adventures in Etymology" is an ongoing writing endeavor (and has been for several years), there are many people deserving of recognition for their inspiration, support, advice, and tolerance. In addition, when such a project evolves into a book-length collection, the list of credits grows. Many people at The University of Alabama Press have been especially helpful and supportive. It was Malcolm M. MacDonald (now retired) who set the publication wheels in motion for *The Clan of the Flapdragon*. His successor as director, Nicole Mitchell, I was happy to learn, shared his enthusiasm for the manuscript. The marketing manager, Judith Knight, provided clear and useful updates as the book lumbered toward release. All in all, my discussions and correspondences with everyone at The University of Alabama Press were positive, productive, and professional; and I am particularly grateful to Marcia Brubeck for her outstanding copyediting of the manuscript and to Beverly Denbow for her care with the proof.

As these Adventures piled up over the years, many friends and acquaintances, colleagues and students, can be thanked and/or blamed for what Dr. Schrapnel has written. My wife, Linda, was instrumental in teaching me how to turn on and use the computer; and being an energetic and versatile librarian, she often uncovered pages and pages of useful data for Dr. Schrapnel's columns. She also sewed the seed for "Martian Warps and Klingon Proverbs." The Vingtiste expertise of Jane Block, Professor of Library Administration at the Ricker Library of Architecture and Art, University of Illinois at Urbana-Champaign, figures mightily in what necessarily became the riddled information on James Ensor in "Tom Ate/Slept Here." It is an essay I read at the 1997 annual conference of the Florida College English Association, thanks to Alan Pratt, of Embry-Riddle Aeronautical University. Professor David Noble, now at the Belmont Campus of Ohio University, introduced me many years ago to the mystique of the wild leek, and from that ramp tour grew "Nosing an Obscure Trope."

Finally, the continuing saga of B. M. W. Schrapnel owes most to Dr. Neal Storrs, editor/publisher of *Oasis*, the small literary magazine that has featured "Adventures in Etymology" for over four years. And in spite of being snubbed by the last few issues of *Writer's Market, Oasis* continues to attract and publish outstanding, serious fiction, poetry, and short theater. Neal Storrs is the proverbial one-in-a-million editor in that he has always been candid and enthusiastic about my Schrapnel submissions, rarely altering a syllable, and often providing sharp ideas for further Adventures, which lie just over the next stack of "reading material." He has also provided selections from *Oasis* writers for our web site, *Welcome to Schrapnelvania*, and he has been a Schrapnel fan and ambassador from the beginning.

# Don't Asp Me!

Except in the herpetology community, the word *asp* is, and has been, used somewhat collectively to refer to any of several poisonous snakes from Africa, Asia, and Europe. Modern snake buffs, however, use *asp* more specifically to denote the Egyptian species of cobra. You know: cobra, that deadly hooded serpent whose bite is fatal most of the time. . . . indeed the cobra, one of the two species reputed to be Cleopatra's instrument of "so long, folks." The other suspect in this glitzy, ancient suicide is the little horned viper, a type of desert sneaky minus the posterior sound effects of its spooky cousin the sidewinder rattlesnake, who slinks and slants across the sandy badlands of the southwestern United States. Are we zero at the bone yet, readers?

Asp is from the Middle English, *aspis*, which filters down from Latin and Greek, and is related to *asparagus* on the etymology vine. And there is much more to asparagus than I will tell you here, besides the microscopic insects that are impossible to remove from the tops. *Aspic*, the word Shakespeare uses for the asp that reputedly bites Cleopatra, may be from sixteenth-century French, although *aspic,* to refer to a serpent, can be found in thirteenth-century English manuscripts. Cobra comes from modern Portuguese, *de capello,* as in "serpent of the hood" (cf. "Hoodunit?" *OASIS,* January–March 1994). Already I have had it with the etymologies here. So let us leave them where they lie and adventure on. Tighten your knee boots.

Now, what once puzzled me, particularly after two bottles of Whatney's Cream Stout and a snifter of Grand Marnier, is how and/or why history is unclear and/or undecided as to the species of snake Cleopatra employed to embark for the happy beguiling ground. Of course, there are those utterly unromantic historians (a few) who still think she used conventional poison stored in a hollowed razor and perhaps pricked herself with a pin to frame any snakes crawling about. Oh, historians. Historians of such persuasion should consult a herpetology text or my neighbor Diedrich, who teaches biology at West Carnage Community College on Tuesday and Thursday mornings. Diedrich's specialty is venomous snakes.

First, consider the behavioral characteristics and things of the two species of accused reptile here. One, the Egyptian cobra—*Naja haje*—is a ferocious and aggressive creature that reaches lengths of six to eight feet. When caged or detained, he can become very agitated and will, upon release or loss of cool, immediately assume a fighting posture, dilating the trademark hood and striking at almost anything that moves or wants to move. By comparison the horned viper—*Cerastes cornutus*—is a weenie, albeit a deadly one. This desert denizen buries itself in the sand to await its prey, often some unsuspecting lizard, insect, or tiny rodent. Cerastes is secretive, shy, and frail. Captives often develop enteritis and suppurative disorders of the mouth, even during short periods of imprisonment. The horned viper rarely exceeds eighteen inches in length.

So what, you ask?

Well, let us just examine the historical evidence of Cleopatra's flashy seppuku, as it is related by Plutarch in his *Lives of the Noble Grecians and Romans,* via the translation from the Greek by James Amyot and from the French by Thomas North. And keep in mind that this edition of Plutarch is Shakespeare's primary source for *Antony and Cleopatra.* And be patient and attentive, because a quiz or contest may follow.

The situation: Cleopatra is pining away in her grandiose mausoleum, believing Marc Antony to be dead, awaiting one of her servants to deliver a basket of figs, in which is concealed on her orders the asp she plans to use to end her life. Plutarch tells us that before the countryman enters the tomb, he opens the basket to show its contents to Caesar's guards outside. Then Plutarch writes (and keep in mind that Plutarch acquired his information from Cleopatra's personal physician, Olympus):

> Some report that this aspic was brought unto her in the basket with figs, that she had commanded them to hide it under the fig-leaves, that when she should think to take out the figs, the aspic would bite her before she should see her: howbeit, that when she would have taken away the leaves for the figs, she perceived it, and said, Art thou here then? And so, her arm being naked, she put it to the aspic to be bitten.
>
> Others say again, she kept it in a box, and that she did prick and thrust it with a spindle of gold, so that the aspic being angered withal, leapt out with great fury, and bit her in the arm. Howbeit few can tell the troth. For they report also, that she had hidden poison in a hollow razor which she carried in the hair of her head: and yet was there no mark seen on her body, or any sign discerned that she was poisoned, neither also did they find this serpent in her tomb. But it was reported only, that there were seen certain fresh steps or tracks where it had gone, on the tomb side toward the sea, and specially by the door side. Some say also, that they found two little pretty bitings in her arm, scant to be discerned: the which it seemeth Caesar himself gave credit unto, because in his triumph he carried Cleopatra's image, with an aspic biting of her arm. And thus goeth the report of her death. (160)

Hmm and no way, say Diedrich and I to the old contention that the snake in the basket was a cobra, because the reported behavior of the guilty reptile is markedly uncharacteristic of that kind of asp. Surely guards' faces would have been bitten. Certainly Cleopatra would not have had to provoke or force a cobra to strike. And if she in fact kept her snake in a box instead, still harassment would not be necessary to make a cobra bite. Recall that the horned viper is a small, frail, and secretive creature that would have remained concealed under the figs and leaves and that gets sick in captivity, developing mouth problems and diarrhea. Coercion might have been necessary to cause this (cerastes) ill asp to inflict a fatal wound.

"What clinches it for me," adds Diedrich the herpetologist, "is the 'certain fresh tracks where it [the asp] had gone.' Clearly the soldiers who discovered the queen's body noticed something odd and identifiable on the scene that definitely indicated the presence of a snake. The *Cerastes cornutus* has that unique sidewinding method of locomotion that leaves in the sand a remarkable trail resembling a parallel series of s-shaped marks. Other species will not leave much of a road sign. Also, the fact that no snake was found at the scene is significant, because a cobra probably would not slither off to hide after being aroused. Cobras are mean and vengeful and sometimes look for trouble. But a little horned viper would have scuttled off and buried itself in the sand, like that species is fond of doing."

Diedrich should know. He once spent a week comatose in an Egyptian hospital, following a field trip that was shortened when he was bitten on the wrist by a cobra that rushed out the open door of an abandoned Peugeot parked along the banks of the lower Nile. Who says Africa is the dark continent no more?

But to return to the Cleopatra caper, no doubt death by cobra bite is something she planned. And an appropriate end it might have been; for the cobra was a symbol of Egyptian deity. Notes W. W. Tarn in *The Cambridge Ancient History,* "The creature deified whom it struck, for it was the divine master of the Sun-god, which raised its head on the crown of Egypt. . . . Once she was alone she arrayed herself in her royal robe and put the asp to her breast; the Sun-god had saved his daughter from being shamed by her enemies and had taken her to himself" (110–11).

Professor Tarn's rehash smacks more of Shakespeare's version than that of recorded history. But the ancient Greek physician Galen reports that cobras were sometimes used to administer a merciful death to condemned prisoners via a bite to the breast. Historical rumors abound of Cleopatra's observance of experiments of this nature, and Shakespeare's text gives credence to them with Caesar's closing remarks that the evidence suggests death by self-inflicted asp bite: "Most probable / That so she died, for her physician tells me / She hath pursued conclusions infinite / Of easy ways to die." Finally, for me as a lover of Shakespeare this slinky revelation turns *Antony and Cleopatra* into a more abysmally tragic tragedy than the Bard himself could have imagined. For if the snake used by Cleopatra to achieve the big snooze is not the royal cobra but a piddling desert viper, then her death is indeed *not* one "fitting for a Princess / Descended of so many royal kings." It is dramatic but terribly pedestrian, because the vehicle she preferred, or planned on, maybe, is not the fabled and sacred asp, *Naja haje*, the Egyptian cobra. It is an "odd worm," as the Clown calls it, that promotes the trick. But the horned viper cannot punch the siren queen's ticket to Egyptian heaven. Only the royal cobra can do that.

Perhaps Cleopatra was too ill educated in the finer points of herpetology to know the difference or was too stressed and desperate to care. And certainly in Shakespeare's genius, if you've seen one asp, you've seen 'em all. That is fine. The amplification of the tragic denouement, though accidental (thanks to modern herpetology), is a whopper. One that really bites.

As usual you overlook additional support for your case. The cobras of ancient Egypt were kept in temples and were tended by holy men. The likelihood that a servant would access such an animal is nearly zero, although a live cerastes or two could be dug up at the base of nearly any sand dune. Too, the difference in the size of the two species also favors the use of a diminutive viper rather than a cobra. *Naja haje* adults are known to guard and defend their young, a trait very rare in snakes.

That makes it very difficult to collect baby cobras. Try putting even a juvenile *Naja haje* in a fig basket. Please.

Joan
San Diego, Calif.

Holy snake droppings, Schrapnel! Notice the observation of the guard in the last scene of *A & C:* "This is an aspic's trail. And these fig leaves / Have slime upon them, such as the aspic leaves / Upon the caves of Nile." Since the horned viper, you say, is known to develop the screaming backdoor trots when held captive for a while, isn't it obvious what that slimy aspic trail really is and who left it? This is not history, of course, but it is evidence. I believe you.

Brad W. Bollingen
Charleston, S.C.

Honest to Christ, who does care whether Cleopatra used a venomous reptile to kill herself? All I know is that it's very hard to duplicate this scene for the stage. The last time I produced and directed *Antony and Cleopatra,* we tried milking, or extracting the venom from, a live cobra so that we could use it safely in the last scene of the play. At dress rehearsal the damn thing killed one actress and paralyzed her understudy. Then it got away and bit a janitor, who took three weeks to die. Cobras have that nasty neurotoxic venom, you know. No one told me that milking a poisonous snake does not necessarily render it even temporarily harmless or that the king cobra we borrowed from the Ross Allen institution (an eight-footer) was the wrong species anyway. No one appreciated the risks I took to achieve verisimilitude.

Bailey S. Archibald
Dade County Correctional Farm

You are indeed an odd egg. One that would astound Shakespeare, I am sure. The moot method of Cleopatra's death, be it the historical or dramatic rendering, is not as important as the fact that she is dead. I do not mean that I am pleased that she is gone, or that I wish she could be reached to clear up the matter, only that I have read your Adventure and now wish I had not done so. But is not life crammed with such regrets and puzzles? And although there are not as many snakes here now in America as there were in ancient Egypt, these reptiles still present a peril to all who dare venture beyond Main Street, or Martin Luther King Boulevard, or whatever the principal vehicular artery of your hometown may be named today. What I would like to see is more literary criticism that takes risks. You enthrall me on some days, and on others you cause me to wish I were a toadstool that could be picked and eaten by my careless, self-centered ex-wife, to work its gloriously painful and deadly havoc upon her fragile body chemistry. Therein, then, wriggles a metaphor even more extralogical than the Cleopatra Paradox you so cryptically dodge. In closing, I want to denounce the environmentalism I once so Thoreausianically embraced and declare simultaneously my intention to drink up or use all of the water in Florida; because the sooner we use it up, the sooner they will leave.

Monroe Nokomis
a.k.a. Chief Thunder Lizard
River-of-Grass, Fla.

FREUD WAS RIGHT

Once upon a warm spring night, in the foothills of the Catskills, I was asked by a university colleague if I would drive her home from an unanimated academic cocktail gathering. Her Cherokee had blown a head gasket in the driveway and was blocking four cars. I said, "It will be a treasure." The party carried on at the home of the dean of academic affairs.

This colleague, Clytemnestra Collingsworth-Manlicher, was a psychology professor who had studied at several Ivy League schools and had spent two years in Kenya as the leader of an underground environmentalist commando team that assassinated elephant poachers free of charge, in the bush, on the spot, or simply on a hunch. To say, then, that she had the uttermost respect of her peers is an understatement comparable to the fateful and final observation of an unknown engineer at Chernobyl: "Sumtink iss wronk!"

Thus when we spied, during the long trip back to town, a bumper sticker on a late-model Lincoln that said "Bop 'til You Drop," sparks and speculation soared.

I passed the car on a straight stretch of two-lane, and we noted that the driver and passenger were young, elegantly dressed women with long blonde hair—details easily visible, for they rode with their dome light burning.

"Dancers and/or jazz aficionados, no doubt," I surmised, as fumes from a host of Boodle's martinis welled in my throat.

"Oh? And why do you say that? I have quite a different evaluation."

Wary of the theories of a devout Freudian, I punched it into etymological mode and explained. "*Bop* is slang for a popular jazz dance of the mid-forties, and jargon for the improvisational genre developed by black jazz artists of that same decade that spawned the dance. Dizzy Gillespie, Charlie Parker, and Billy Eckstine, to name a few, were prominent boppers, if you will."

She grinned and shook her head. "Nearly everything nowadays is, or becomes, sexual. Those women are tarts, sluts, nymphos at best. 'Fornicate until you faint' is what they really mean."

"Clyde," I declared, asquirm with anticipation.

"B.M.," she sighed. "Get with the program. Freud was right. Do you have any ibuprofen?"

Alas, the slings and arrows of discourse, I delivered the suddenly migrained Clytemnestra to port without further disaccord or fantasy. I rushed home to my reference library, where I thrashed through slang dictionaries and music encyclopedias until four in the morning.

In Penguin's *Encyclopedia of Popular Music,* I read, "Boppers often flatted the fifth note of a chord, inventing short routes between keys: Eddie Condon said, 'We don't flatten our fifths, we drink 'em.' (But Igor Stravinsky had used flatted fifths in 1910.)"

And according to J. David, *bop,* in student slang, means to date many different people. In drug culture a *bop* is a pill or a hit. In Partridge, *bop* means to hit, as in "bopped him on the nut," or head.

Recalling that a German root of our infamous f-word is *ficken* (to hit or strike), I began to see how Clyde's interpretation came to pass. For it is Chapman, in *The New Dictionary of American Slang,* who contends that *bop* (along with *boff* and *screw*) is supplanting the f-word as obscenity most often uttered in reference to that aspect of sexual lingo. Jeepers, I say.

Bonk underwent a similar etymological mutation, since it originally meant "to hit resoundingly," but is now a synonym for the sex act in young people's slang and journalese. *Bonkers,* however, may yet refer to madness or be the plural agent noun of *bonk.*

Now, if all of this does not wheeze for air enough, remember the country music hit recorded by Dan Seals, wherein he warbles, "I want to bop with you baby, all night long"? And while the former England Dan seems to have dancing on his mind—for they are going down to the local armory to hear a hot band—should we not wonder whether carpe diem is afoot there, with slithery euphemism wriggling alongside?

Then, of course, there was the fifties rock idol The Big Bopper, whose baby knew what he liked.

Clyde was right.

Bop this, idiot! I grow weary of all this sex, sex, sex. *Bop,* in the language of most normal people, still means music and dance. A good bop on your nut (either) will probably help your outlook. You must be a throwback to those days when all men were pigs.

Rocko S.
Middlesex, N.J.

Your usually perverse etymological preoccupations suggest that you are a deranged fraud with a one-track mind the size of a martini garnish. I suspect that you still sleep with your mother.

Alice B. Curb, Ed.D.
Count Dracula Community College
Herbivore, Md.

Your work qualifies you for unparalleled scholarly distinction, particularly those notable efforts (veiled as they must be so as not to offend some) to rid our native tongue of word taboos.

Our institution would be honored if you would speak at our 1993 spring commencement. Your *bop* piece was a gem.

Dean S. M. Gordonkofski, Ph.D.
Missouri School for the Sexually Gifted

I did ask you . . . never to use even a scrap of any of our conversations in your syndicated column, for any reason, ever! You have, as the world now knows, betrayed me. You will not be as fortunate as, say, Rushdie, has been. —Seriously, Clyde

THE CLAN OF THE FLAPDRAGON

Sure it's old news, Bush's Brouhaha. But it's the diction, you warped word watchers out there. The scene is a meeting room in a Frank Lloyd Wright–style student union building somewhere on campus in the southeastern United States. A young veteran of Operation Desert Storm (male infantry) spouts to about two dozen grunge-scene undergrads, "We showed that Hussein and his henchmen that you just can't go around and flapdragon any friends of the great U.S. of A."

Sure we did, but *flapdragon?*

Now, there is a verb, among other things. And if you flounder about *Webster's Unabridged,* you will find it—*flapdragon:* "to swallow or devour quickly; to snatch and swallow at a single gulp, as a player of flapdragon." Thus *flapdragon,* the verb, comes from the compound noun of the same spelling, which refers to an old drinking game wherein players snatch floating raisins from bowls of flaming liquor and eat the fruit.

From Dr. Johnson's Dictionary to the *OED,* this is the consensus. The fruit bobs in the booze, and the contestant must grab it, pop it into the mouth and swallow. Notes in G. B. Harrison's edition of Shakespeare, however, call it differently. For in *Love's Labour's Lost* we find:

MOTH. [aside to Costard] They have been at a great feast of languages, and stolen the scraps.

COST. Oh, they have lived long on the alms basket of words. I marvel thy master has not eaten thee for a word; for thou art not so long by the head as honorificabilitudinitatibus. Thou art easier swallowed than a flap-dragon.

Harrison here defines *flapdragon* as "a lighted raisin floated on liquor which had to be swallowed." Similarly, when *flapdragon* jumps out in *2 Henry IV* ("Drinks of candles' ends for flapdragons, and rides the wild mare"), the editor claims *flapdragon* denotes "lighted candles floated in a glass of drink. The drinker must drink without burning himself." Furthermore, in a footnote to a passage in *The Winter's Tale,* Harrison explains that "Swallowing flap-dragons (lighted raisins floating on liquor) was a winter amusement."

Wassailers of America must wonder, then, which is it? Do you first light the raisins or ignite the liquor? And does it actually matter? A high-test brandy was the usual spirit of choice for flap-dragon, so would not a burning raisin fire the brandy (from the Dutch, *brundewijn,* for burnt wine) anyway? Probably is the answer.

More quizmatic, though, are two questions: where and/or how in Hades did such a game originate? and why did folks play it? To answer query 2 first, the Rev. T. F. Thiselton Dyer, in the 1883 edition of *Folk-Lore of Shakespeare,* explains: "Gallants used to vie with each other in drinking off flap-dragons to the health of their mistresses—which were sometimes even candles' ends, swimming in brandy or other strong spirits, whence, when on fire, they were snatched by the mouth and swallowed."

Women, of course. And how about those misplaced modifiers?

The name *flapdragon,* it is suggested, comes from the German *Schnapps* (spirit) and *Drache* (dragon), making it equivalent to Fire-Spirit. *Snapdragon,* by the way, became synonymous with *flapdragon* in the early eighteenth century. According to John Ayto, snapdragon is "a party game which involved picking raisins out of a bowl of burning brandy and eating them while they were still alight—the allusion being of course to the dragon's fire-breathing habits."

So we are not talking flowers here, botany buffs.

The various heroic rituals of the Fire-Spirit are traced by

Frazer and others (like Norm and Cliff) to perhaps the centuries surrounding the composition and memorization of *Beowulf,* give or take a few hundred years. In *Blickling Homilies* (colloquial tendencies), A.D. 971, there is the saga of the invasion and brief conquest of Britain by the fierce Nordic-Germanic tribe known as Weltzschmutz Swine-Breath. The Swine-Breath ruled for less than a week and were consumed almost as mysteriously by a great fire. According to the Old to Middle English text translated by the late Monmouth M. Tillis:

> The Weltzschmutz, to celebrate their conquest, gathered in a great natural amphitheater outside of what is now Liverpool, where they passed around hundreds of large, clay bowls of flaming liquor, in which floated the many severed and diced finger joints of their slain enemies. For several days and nights they reveled and played a game similar to the Celtic "Bobbing-for-Apples." The warriors plunged their grizzled faces into the fiery bowls to see who could gobble the most niblets of humanity. There was much drinking and head-slapping and beard-dousing, and the festivities they called the rites of The Clan of the Flapdragon, for the Draco was their deity and their guiding spirit, and the symbol of Nordic-Germanic Capitalism. But as the Swine-Breath frenzy mounted, and the topers became more of the clumsy spirit of their fiery gods, bowls began to spill everywhere. Soon the entire camp was afire and the drunken victors, so drunk, were helpless to flee. A pyre of such magnitude arose that it could be seen in St. Augustine, and the conquering Weltzschmutz were consumed one and all. The lone remnant of their short rule is a charred, stone tablet, whereon is carved in frantic hand the names of the leaders of The Clan of the Flapdragon—Sven the Scarred, Hemglob the Hairless, Blind Gogar and Lars the Lipless.

While the validity of this very ancient account is almost totally dubious—liquor of flammable proof and raisin technology nearly unknown in the century of the tale's supposed date—it is clear, nevertheless, that the origin of the old drinking game flapdragon (snapdragon) predates what is usually believed by mixological historians to be the earliest known time of the distillation of alcoholic beverages. But Vikings and such, to be sure, were notorious for keeping secrets about their social habits, such as the making and hoarding of brandy. History says that various deranged orders of monks were the first to do this, to distill. Look again.

In conclusion, *honorificabilitudinitatibus* is old Latin denoting "in the condition of being loaded with horns." The word is a scholar's joke, as it is the longest word in the Latin tongue. Could anyone ever have bested Shakespeare in a spelling bee, do you think?

Flapdoodle! Look that one up, lexicographic loon. The game of snapdragon, according to the *OED,* is of Christian antecedent and is usually played at Christmas time. Are we reading the same reference book, or is your old LSD habit haunting you again? Cf. Swift's *Tale of the Tub:* "He bore a strange kind of appetite to snap-dragon, and to the livid snuffs of a burning candle." Thus I challenge you to a game of flapdragon—one-inch candles in Grand Marnier. The first one to reach ten wins.

Elvis Peebles
SUNY-Duluth

You should not have played down in your column the dangerous aspects of flapdragon. My cousin Mario lost his right eyebrow and lashes in a game once. And if it catches on with those always impressionable and romantic college students, we could have a lot of fires on campus.

Lola Defazio
Princeton, N.J.

Your piece on flapdragon was déjà vu all over again for me. I remember playing the game at the airport in Tokyo in 1970. We were returning from Nam, my army buddies and I. One of them suddenly had a bad combat flashback, and he threw the burning bowl at a waitress. He's still in a Japanese jail, and the waitress is a congresswoman in California. What do you think it all means?

Gary Deere
Sacramento, Calif.

The way I understand it, the name *flapdragon* refers to the eyelid of the ancient mythological beast. In other words, the flap that covered the dragon's eye. In Bubonic mythology, the flapdragon is a coveted part of the animal because it can be dropped into any vessel, vat, river, or lake and may cause the liquid to explode into flames. The great Bubonic king Blobath is said to have defeated the invading Curds from Germany by tossing a flapdragon into the river Ichsola as the Curd army tried to cross. The motif takes various forms throughout Indo-European lore, and my son the musician says it is a recurring theme in the early records of Black Sabbath.

C. Brutus Ulrich, Ph.D.
SMU

Here's a word for you, Schrapnel—*dungorificabilitudinitatibus.*
Brevity is the soul of spit, and so on.

Candy
Vegas

Scholarship, Mischief, and Sleaze

Ezra Pound is a name with which I have always wished to uncork one of my columns, not so much because the name is both biblical and weighty (for I am neither blazingly Christian nor terribly fat), but because that poet looms in the literary crannies of many memories as a symbol of both genius and booby. As G. Quentin Riggs of the University of Southeastern West Virginia observes, in his denounced biography of E.L.P., "I mean, how is it he writes such great poems, knows so many important writers, then makes radical broadcasts for the pizza man and gets his derrière tossed in the cage?"

Thus *poon*, a unisyllabic much in sound like the surname of the poet (as well as his middle one—Loomis), we all know to be any of several types of East Indian trees whose seeds yield a bitter oil. *Poon* may also denote the oil of any of those trees. And while Tang is the Chinese dynasty that ruled southeast Asia from the seventh to the tenth centuries, tang is also the small end, or tongue, of a knife or sword that fastens into a handle. As verb, *tang* means to ring loudly.

Now, how in the bloody hell *poontang* is synonymous with sexual intercourse, to quote my young nephew away at a private parochial school, "beats the poop out of me!" But you can peruse it all in *Webster's Unabashed,* Partridge's slang volume, or the Famous Grouse.

Dictionaries all over, nevertheless, are in mootness about the etymological origin of *poontang.* Is it Chinese, French (cf. *putain,* or prostitute), or Philippine, as translated by the U.S. Army? And why did the word originally imply copulation with "a coloured woman?" What colour? And how can it be that *poontanger* is the penis of a Canadian lumberman?

Bewildering, is it not?

One must suspect, then, that some drunken and/or drug-driven Freudian pedagogue—from his copyediting room overlooking the sinewy boulevards of London or New York—has committed lexicographic tampering at a high editorial level, which he guessed would never be questioned by the plebeians in the print shop. Thus whimsy flies, and uncertainty remains. For scholarship, like all the myriad livelihoods, is hardly devoid of mischief and sleaze. Poontang is proof—more to come on this subject in a fortnight or two.

Your etymologies are, to be kind, terribly suspect, Doctor. And I think you must sleep with your mother.

Alice B. Curb, Ed.D.
Count Dracula C.C.
Herbivore, Md.

You blithering, shit-for-brains asshead! *Poontang* appears in an unpublished Hemingway short story, "Nick and the Carrot Stick," that is locked in the Kennedy Library collection so that boobies like you won't spill instant coffee on the manuscript. To put it in paraphrase that even you might follow, Nick uses *poontang* onomatopoeically to denote the sound he hears when Toby Atwater's nephew shoots his pneumatic BB gun at the empty pot still his uncle once used to make exotic liqueurs. This predates all that you claim in your column, quagmire cranium. You should attempt some thorough research occasionally instead of sleeping with your sister.

Elvis Peebles
SUNY, Duluth

Shakespeare never employed *poontang* as a noun.

A. C. Bradley
London

"And then Ezra Pound leaped from his stool and shouted to the lieutenant, 'Take your puny tank and point its guns at some other poet.' "

Undoubtedly you are aware of this anecdote, but your liberal application of it wheezes.

Armand Desantis
Rome and Genoa

 HOODUNIT?

William F. Scarlet's lately heralded and long-awaited biography of Robin Hood begets new questions and imputations about the slang etymology of *hood,* often claimed to be an abbreviation or contraction of *hoodlum,* which supposedly originated in San Francisco around 1871 to describe "a youthful street rowdie; a loafing youth of dangerous proclivities." It is there, and more of course, in *The Oxford English Dictionary.*

The origin of *hoodlum,* firstly, is variously assumed. Hood may have been the surname of a prominent Frisco gang leader. Or it could be a short version of Muldoon spelled backward—suggest some opiate-riddled lexicographers—changed by a hyperopic typesetter who took the *n* of *noodluM* for an *h.* I am not fabricating here. The latter theory assumes that most hoods are (or were) Irish, perhaps, and that their jovial, lovable St. Patrick's Day hijinks are a smokescreen for antisocial and criminal enterprises. In addition and contradiction, there is the recent prejudice out of Florida that most hoods are Afro-American or Hispanic; and this hypothesis, as you read, elicits much assent in Germany. And German, finally, is the most likely source for *hoodlum.* You see, there is the Bavarian *hodalum* (scamp) and/or *hydelum* (disorderly). As Hugh Rawson observes in his *Wicked Words,* "Aside from the linguistic parallel, this explanation has the virtue of fitting the ethnic data, since Germans seem to have constituted the largest non-English speakers in San Francisco around 1870."

But let us leave our hoods in San Francisco for a few paragraphs and return to William F. Scarlet's *Robin Hood: An Unauthorized Biography.* Scarlet maintains that Robin Hood was born Robert Fitzooth, in Locksley, Nottinghamshire, in 1160 and later became the Earl of Huntingdon. Fitzooth's much orally publicized falling out with the crooked and infamous Sheriff of Nottingham, one Uriah Legree, is said to have occurred over disputed mineral rights to a beaver dam. It is the proverbial long story again, resplendent in fire-tipped arrows, false bridges, and fur coats. Eventually, Fitzooth denounced the political system, the English Forestry Service, and law and order as well, illegally changed his name, and—well, you can guess the rest of the rising action.

Some of Scarlet's nearly dubious accounts of the early years of Robin Hood are corroborated by, or are plagiarized from, *Funk and Wagnalls Standard Dictionary of Folklore, Mythology, and Legend.* And that is delectable. However, *F&W* also buys into the belief of Francis James Child, nineteenth-century Harvard's distinguished ballad scholar, that Robin Hood "is absolutely a creation of the ballad-muse." Destined to burn until court injunction day is thus the question as to who lies entombed in Kirklees Hall, Yorkshire, where the bronze plate reads:

Robin Hood
1160–1247
famous rural philanthropist & archer
bled to death by a treacherous woman

Hood's bow and arrow are displayed there also. So is it not improbable that Robin Hood, the man and the grave, is a hoax? Scarlet is a natural believer in the best sense that Robert Fitzooth, Earl of Huntingdon, did succumb to the throes of political disenchantment and a kind of pre-Thoreausian rapture to become the legendary merry man of Sherwood Forest who pilfered the wealthy that he might endow the pauperized. But nevermind the Deconstruction. You may scan the accounts in the early chapters of *Robin Hood: An Unauthorized Biography.*

More immediate and unnerving are the last three chapters of the book, wherein William F. Scarlet's nose for investigative literary scholarship is at its runniest. There he blows the sheets off of an etymological cover-up that began over two centuries ago and involves the unlikely likes of Alexander Pope, Washington Irving, Noah Webster, and Cromwell Philpot. Perhaps the participation in a literary hoodwink by Irving, that most shameless copycat of American letters, will not surprise many readers, knowing as they must how he appropriated word for word from German folktales for his short stories and copied from the naturalist William Bartram for a sketch or two. Even at the junior college level, such dishonesty is an automatic F for the course and possible expulsion from the institution. Omission from future Norton anthologies seems the least that Washington Irving deserves now, but wait. There is yet more slime on this American bag.

It begins with Alexander Pope's edition of Shakespeare (1775), which was the only copy of the Bard's work that Irving owned. And as scholars know, Pope was one of the premier corruptors of Shakespeare, basing his "revisions" on his self-appointed good taste and warped Classicism. This deformed little houser of Great Danes (as in canines) was a known denouncer of English folklore, for reasons even the most prurient psychological critics blush to print or discuss. Pope revered ultimately Ye Olde Classics, which must explain why his edition of Homer is superior to his Shakespeare, who tapped oftentimes the cask of folklore for some of his most inebrious plots and metaphors.

Thus when Pope reads in a rare Shakespeare manuscript from which he worked—

POLONIUS. [to Ophelia] Read on
this book,
That show of such an exercise may color
Your loneliness. Ah-yuck! Ah-yuck! This will
Put an ape in his hood!

—the Popester scribbles in the margin, with unabashed disregard for the sanctity of the manuscript, "hood! hood! for shame, tis reminder of the harsh, dirty folk-tales of Robin H." And so Alexander Pope removed the folkloristic allusion/idiom, "Put an ape in his hood," along with the chortles.

Similarly, this Neo-Classical gas scratched Falstaff's lewdity about "the bone in my master's hood" from *2 Henry IV.* Such a colloquialism, in both plays, is delightful comic relief. The phrase in *Hamlet* means "to befool." Falstaff's context, while tantalizing to Freudians, most probably refers to a blow on the head and a resulting concussion, or even the biting of the Big One, to employ another crude euphemism that Pope would reject.

Washington Irving's part in this corruption was made possible many decades later unknowingly by Sir Walter Scott, who somehow acquired those rare Shakespeare/Pope folios for his personal library but never examined them. They might still be a part of the Scott estate had he not allowed the popular American "writer" full rout of his volumes. Irving "borrowed" the Shakespeare folios, and saw what Pope did, but because he idolized Pope and misunderstood Shakespeare (perhaps too was reluctant to draw attention to his own fascination with folktales), yes! Irving chose not to go public with the scandalous discovery. "Obviously," conjects Scarlet, "Scott was not aware that Irving was such a creep."

Scarlet's sources in his inquiry become, at this point, fogged. But they nevertheless move along with Ouija-board clarity. Most remarkable is Irving's unpublished letter to William Cullen Bryant, wherein the Washmeister discloses this old and secret tampering through six pages of guilt-laden prose, much of it his own. Bryant's reply, however, is a curt one: "Is it the rhum again, Irv?"

And indeed it is all quite unbelievable until Scarlet comes to his crowning find regarding the original draft of *Henry VIII*, believed to be Shakespeare's last-written surviving play. Again, it is the same folio that Pope "edited" and Irving perused a century later at Scott's place. And in act 5, scene 2, there is the following song sung by Doctor Butts (the King's physician) that is omitted by Pope, and consequently by all future editions of Shakespeare, because the manuscript "disappeared" following Pope's project.

Of Robin Hood and his merry hoods
There is but one, a monk.
His counsel is an anchor
That curtails the hoods' amuck.

The revelation here, William Scarlet explains, is twofold: (1) Pope removed, as the mood swayed him, many references in Shakespeare to Robin Hood, and the very word *hood*. Who cares why, really. It is just deranged, dishonest, hack editing. (2) It was Shakespeare, and not some nineteenth-century American journalist, who coined *hood* in the slang sense to denote a gang member something like the hoodlums who rode with Robin Hood. This seeming reemergence into the common language of *hood,* centuries after the Bard's coinage, is now further testimony to the need for an origins and dissemination theory of folklore that lies somewhere in between polygenesis and diffusion. Look those up in your Brunvand intro to folklore text.

Oh! But do not turn to a poem yet; the etymological scam does not end with the tasteless and sophomoric Washington Irving. You see, those Shakespeare manuscripts still exist, says Scarlet, and they have been scrutinized by some scholarly heavies whose disregard for the true fabric of literary history is, yes, distressful. For none less than that premier lexicographer Noah Webster is known to have gasped at Irving's "borrowed" folio in the year of his death (Webster's), 1843. But knowing the damage that disclosure could wreak on the Washmeister's reputation, and that of Pope, gasp is all that Noah managed. So in accordance with Webster's will, his family bought, and locked away, all of Irving's notes and editions that he acquired in England or scarfed elsewhere.

Enter, a generation later, a renegade cousin of the Websters, Cromwell Philpot, who was granted access to the Webster estate records when James A. H. Murray appointed him to compile the H section of the *OED.* And while Noah Webster remained mum from a sense of love and loyalty, Philpot's reason for continuing the cover-up was exquisite hatred. That is, Cromwell Philpot hated Shakespeare, as evidenced, says Scarlet, by his violent outbursts and dismissals from several of A. C. Bradley's lectures at Glasgow. Moreover, Philpot was notorious for holding up a placard that declared "the bard's a bum!" whenever the name of Shakespeare entered the air. So you will not find Shakespeare cited in the *OED*'s slang etymologies of *hood.*

Now, if all of this is not the most glorious crock of nonfiction feces you have ever read, or will read, good grief! behold how William F. Scarlet came to unravel it all. Clued was he, he writes, through a painting by the German Expressionist Max Beckmann (1884-1950) entitled *Begin the Beguine.* Forget Cole Porter here. Scarlet recalls, "Beckmann's little-known painting startled me in an almost paranormal manner and haunted me until I pursued a road presumably not taken by lexicographers or etymologists heretofore. Since *beguine,* as Beckmann employs it, refers to the rumbalike dance of Martinique, and remembering that *beguine* is also old French for hood (although today it can be *beguin,* meaning an infatuation or fancy), I followed a mnemonic irrelevancy of sorts. For Beckmann's painting contains, to the right of the dancers, a demure, Robin Hood–like figure clad in Lincoln green coat and dark tights, much like those that Olivier must have donned for his dismal, posturing Hamlet. Beckmann, during his brief study of linguistics under Cromwell Philpot at Oxford, writes in his memoirs that he was compelled to flee England when it was discovered that on successive nights he and a young woman stole into Philpot's office to use his couch, and stumbled into evidence of a long-running plot in the lexicographic sphere designed to dampen the genius of Shakespeare, or at least muffle it."

Is not the denouement terribly bald now?

Scarlet was led to comb Beckmann's diary by a cryptic detail in his art. As to why Beckmann never blew ye olde whistle, Scarlet notes that Cromwell Philpot's reputation for violence, his preference for fisticuffs and/or flogging instead of discourse and debate, no doubt frightened the timid artist. Philpot was known to kick the ass of anyone who spoke out against him. His colleagues feared him and eventually ceased to question or challenge him on anything he wrote or said. He was a scholar hood. And he would have at least killed Beckmann if the young would-be artist at that time dared betray him or try to smear him. Therefore Beckmann only chanced that left-field clue in one of his paintings, hoping that it would trigger the curiosity of the right scholar into deeper meditation and research into the conspiracy involving Robin Hood/Shakespeare et al.

I know.

But at least *Robin Hood: An Unauthorized Biography* is not another of those celebrity exposés dripping with secret lust, drugs, and a forbidden appetite for children. So in ultimate conclusion, anxiety over the correct pronunciation of the title of this essay may be relieved by William and Mary Morris's report that genuine hoods pronounce *hood* to rhyme with *brood.* Now, readers, are there any fleeing squids aswim in your consciousness? Now can you see why the *New York Review of Books* never commissions me to contribute?

If you happened to see Mel Brooks's last classic about Robin Hood that he called "Men in Tights" you could of seen them use *hood* to mean hood the way you said it means, and the movie also takes place before the journalist are suppose to of made it up in San Francisco. I think your right and I wish they'd quit printing so many letters that make you sound like some kind of idiot. Your fan

Gerrard Mellon
Pittsburgh, Pa.

While William F. Scarlet's scholarship is frowned upon with near unanimity by the combined departments of English of the Ivy League schools, you at least raise a clever point of conclusion in your essay; namely that the American publishing industry is top-heavy with both fiction and nonfiction that is trivial, trashy, and trite. Although minuscule, it is the first sane and gutsy innuendo I have read by you, and at last I look forward to meeting you—my biological father—during my next semester break. Will be in touch again soon.

Claude W. Schrapnel
Dartmouth University

My late grandfather, Cromwell Philpot, Ph.D., was not the unprincipled bully that W. F. Scarlet would like us to believe him to be. I am not sure where you stand on Scarlet's opium dream masquerading as scholarship, but family honor dictates that I must seek out the both of you and right these wrongs you have printed. And if I were your editors, I would watch my rear as well.

Laertes Philpot II
Fargo, N.D.

The Feminist Community commends you for an essay finally devoid of any slurs aimed at us. This doesn't mean that we have removed your name from our top ten list of degenerate chauvinist swine—once a pig, always a pig—but we do encourage you to continue on an artistic path that has no cultural or spiritual potholes. Please accept and employ the enclosed packet of condoms as an additional token of our hopes and best wishes.

Cordelia M. Barthelme-Peggs
NOW, Sacramento, Calif.

As one who has studied, taught, and revered for four decades the work of Washington Irving, the true Father of American

Literature, I am shocked by your derogatory accusations of plagiarism and the suggestion that the greatness of early American letters is a myth. We have, it is true, our great men in America: not a city but has an ample share of them. I have mingled among them in my time and have been almost withered by the shade into which they cast me; for there is nothing so baleful to a small man as the shade of a great one, particularly the great man of a city. You, Dr. Schrapnel, I suspect are unable to cast any shadow; and do we not all know what such a creature that denotes?

Irving L. Washington-Scott,
Provost Marshall (ret.)
Bracebridge Visitation Academy
Albany, N.Y.

(Editorial Note: The second and third sentences of the above letter are lifted word for word from Washington Irving's "The Author's Account of Himself," published in New York by C. S. Van Winkle in 1819. It appears that Irving's methods remain contagious. So avoid him. B.M.W.S.)

# CLEOPATRA'S BILGE

An ancient mentor, Dr. Elwood Vance Vindicuff, at one time the youngest emeritus professor ever appointed at Yale, wrote me recently in response to my long column entitled "Hoodunit?" My essay is, in large part, a review of William F. Scarlet's controversial *Robin Hood: An Unauthorized Biography,* wherein Scarlet declares that he has discovered an etymological cover-up concerning the slang origin of *hood* that runs from Alexander Pope to the eccentric Cromwell Philpot and hence through the *OED* Itself. Because Professor Vindicuff's extensive views on the Scarlet book are so fresh and annoying, I think it fruitful and wise to give him some space here by way, mostly, of paraphrase. E.V.V. is no rookie left-winger but a hybrid deconstructionist whose latest work, *Willa Cather and the Masturbation Motif as Ethnic Angst,* received the 1989 Jock Derrière Award for the most deconstructive use of Deconstruction by a New England scholar.

Ergo, Dr. Vindicuff finds a veiled but urgent sociocultural semaphore in Scarlet's *Robin Hood*—a moral, if you will. The lesson centers on the example of the late Cromwell Philpot, that renegade lexicographer who reportedly thugged on those who opposed him and his work in any way. He took no jokes. And because of this violent and hostile man, a scary injustice was further perpetrated upon Western letters for nearly three centuries. Something like that.

"Cromwell Philpot is a social text," says Dr. Vindicuff, "that cannot be shunned and disregarded. He is the axiomatic, historical antecedent to the often ignored motif that the liberal arts does have in its ranks some insidious and dangerous elements."

Get 'em, Elwood!

According to Dr. Vindicuff, you see, there is in Scarlet's *RH* (most particularly in the Philpot yarn) a lesson that higher education and its satellites must not be blind to. Fact is, the liberal arts contain some perilously dishonest people—scholars and so on of Machiavellian, even Hitlerian, temperament who are as capable of criminal deceit and arch violence as any hood in the neighborhood, any jungle mercenary, drug lord lieutenant, lumber company owner, or real estate developer. And because scholars and professors are typically such sheep, those rare wolves of the environment can ravage the education food chain to any gluttonous degrees they desire. Yes, even supposedly wimpy and specialized fields, such as lexicography, etymology, and textual criticism, harbor unprincipled villains to whom even Shakespeare is a mere cheekful of junk food.

Moreover, then, all of the hoopla-doopla across American university campuses over curriculum content in the humanities—do we stick with the traditional canon (Great Books) or open the liberal, multicultural wickets to let in pop and ethnic literature (Louis L'Amour to Alice Walker, Wang Chung Flu to Frito Louise Fernandez)—well, what the hell, huh?

Oh, come on, now, E.V.V. declares in a way. Awaken and whiff the carnage. It is truly a wrong question or at least a species of the untutored herring, perhaps not quite red, but certainly pink and broiling.

"We are indeed what we read," Dr. Vindicuff reminds us. "And embrace it or not, it is a cluttered democracy in which we sing this boisterous swan song to the students of the arts."

All right.

And given the growing and real dangers in and out of American institutions—the muggery, druggery, and murders—E. V. Vindicuff tells us to believe in the proof of stark empiricism, that the really practical curriculum adjustment necessitates the integration (at least into the English major) of required courses such as "Acute Martial Arts," "Expository Handgun," and "Concealed Cutlery Management."

"After all," adds the Vinmeister, "was it not Milton, in the unpublished sequel to *Areopagitica*—the sweetly cryptic *Thus Spake*

Misanthropos—who observes that mankind, in the close and growing numbers that he is, is an uncomfortable and unpredictably violent creature? A little population growth is a dangerous thing? Crowds breed antisocial backlash, and broad territory is everything? If not Milton, then assuredly Thomas Malthus."

Darned if Schrapnel knows for certain.

Whether Dr. Vindicuff's warning packs enough hysteria to assure him a desk on the same floor with Al Bloom, Rick Marius, and Roger Kimball—on that big Curriculum Development Committee in the sky—well, let us simply hope for the proverbial best, readers, students, my fellow writers and educators. As for this etymologist/scholar/writer/teacher/model railroader, I believe that if you avoid Miami, New York, Chicago, and Los Angeles for starters, you may go ahead and eat more red meat.

⚜ The Protean Obscenity and His Sister

F——, with the possible exception of *c*——, is indeed the most reviled (as it should be) of our taboo words. It is one of a fistful of dirty terms that is rarely seen fully in print in any civilized or serious work. For a scholarly and convincing argument as to why men, and especially women, should snub such language, read Barbara Lawrence's old and famous essay, "Four-Letter Words Can Hurt You," a very accessible example of etymological study.

But all revulsion and taste aside for a moment, what is most striking about *f*—— is the word's unabashed utility. Consider the declaration of the late Edward Abbey's eloquent ecowarrior, George Washington Hayduke (of *The Monkey Wrench Gang*), after he has poured sugar into the fuel tank of the bulldozer: "The f——ing f——ers f——ed."

Hayduke's vernacular, seasoned as it was by a tour of Vietnam, should impress even the most everyday English teacher. That is, notice that the f-word is employed correctly as a modifier, noun, and verb in the same sentence. Hemingway knew that it could be, as did James Joyce. And no doubt Shakespeare, the Baron of Bawd, in a more liberal literary climate, could have floored his audiences with usage variations on the f-word.

So, as for the most interesting and well-documented review of the f-word through literary history, nothing can top Hugh Rawson and his *Wicked Words* (Crown, 1989). This reference book contains over ten pages of background, anecdote, example, and legal history of one of the English language's forever censored and most euphemized terms, the f-word. You should not be surprised either that it has taken many writers (among them Norman Mailer) years to learn to spell the f-word correctly.

As for the c-word, Rawson (oh, what better surname can there be for a lexicographer who specializes in researching vile speech) gives it six pages of etymology and usage while maintaining that *c*—— is even more tabooed than the f-word. What?!? Evidence for this point, Rawson claims, is that there are more euphemisms for the c-word and the fact that it is generally not spoken by men or women before adulthood. Right?

In conclusion, there is the claim of the internationally benign taxidermist Wolf B. Crane that if the c-word ever wriggles into mainstream dictionaries, the likeness of his wicked stepmother will adjoin it in the margin. Crane is not right, but we all know what marginalia might accompany the f-word if an identical lexicographic fate upends it.

Beatnik poems that contain the f-word are found in modern poetry books that you have to buy for college classes like introduction to literature and maybe the second semester of freshman composition. Such poems are full of sentence fragments. But if the f-word and the c-word get into dictionaries, I don't appreciate it. Or the idea of poetry coming to this. And I especially don't like my professors who make us read and talk about them. Why can't writers like yourself just ignore the possibilities?

Maisy Killian
Ozark, Mo.

The possibility that both the f- and c-word may appear someday in regular dictionaries is another symptom of the literary apocalypse that threatens Western letters. Surely it is notable that Zane Grey, Louis L'Amour, Jane Austen, Mary J. Grosbeak, and Fergus McDougalhenny never saw the need to employ such harsh language in their novels. Nor do I recall such smut in Samuel Richardson, although I have yet to finish *Clarissa*.

Fonda Louise Sheets
Bangor, Maine

You know . . . don't choo . . . that one day no one will be shocked by anything. . . . F or C or the dead kid on the tree . . . , people just get shockproof from the boob tube and friends. . . . wheez all going down, man, . . . so grab a branch and make friends with a bird!

the dark poet
berkeley

 # PRUFROCKERY

Prufrockery is a word I coin to designate the multifaceted social lameness displayed occasionally to often by some middle-aged yuppies with liberal arts degrees. You remember, J. Alfred Prufrock is T. S. Eliot's famous, fearful wimp who cannot decide whether to pop the question or pop his arteries, as it was explicated to my undergraduate intro to lit class once. Al is a lot like Hamlet in that his indecision holds him in a wheelspin. But unlike the prince, he never jumps ship and reaches the proverbial breaking point, to wreak carnage upon his social disorder. Just think about it.

One is afflicted with prufrockery if she no-shows a job interview because, "Well, gee, I really don't think I want to be a garbage woman, I mean, a sanitary engineer anyway. I mean, what will people say? And so what if it pays twenty dollars an hour, and the twins are going off to college in the fall?"

Prufrockery, you see, is not a male gender phenom. It can stymie even the most matriarchal wench.

Prufrockery has you by the thigh hairs when you refuse another snifter of Napoleon before midnight because you remember what such similar stuff did to Dylan Thomas finally. You think of his besotted, puking near corpse, in writhing coitus with the Eternal Footperson, on the floor of the White Horse Tavern. Aah legend! It is such a vivid intimidator, the Great Deluger on parades.

At last, prufrockery has nailed you when you buy a giant telescopic lens for your 35mm but don't use it to Kodacolor the young mermaids as they strut the white sand in their ensembles. In fact, you are certainly in the throes of prufrockery when you will not dare walk the beach with the whole phallic thing around your neck, fearing comparison to the Ancient Mariner or some other old hippie. Ludicrous, you say?

Well, of course it is! But would you want your daughter to marry J. Alfred Prufrock? Or do you think that T. S. Eliot worried about Philistine opinions like yours? Do you?

All digression and red herring aside now, prufrockery is something to take up cudgels against. It is debilitating, for certain. But there is a sort of nostrum, a cure to which Eliot alludes in his eximious long poem. And this saving formula is as old as Catullus— carpe diem! Or gather ye rosebuds, etcetera, etcetera. So go at each day with throttle unbent and open for business, but pause at times to read some good verse, at least in snatches. Start with Marvell (as in Andrew, not comics) and his sapient "To His Coy Mistress." Have a ball.

Once again you suck for air, word-wringer! In the 1939 novelette by neolesbian Nazi Symbolist Hildegard Van Munchkin Cross—entitled *Chastity Belt Blues*—there lies the following: "Barnhardt playfully kicked Mordred's Siamese kitten, sipped on the divinely iced rye in the crystal, old-fashioned glass, then queerly scorned, 'Now, you do not wish to go to Club Erotica! You should not be seen there, you say. You are afraid to get jiggered again because Paulette may disapprove. Really, Mordred! This prufrockery of yours makes me want to ——!' " Thus you have coined nothing, lying, slobbering phoney. Try reading a book one day, instead of drooling over back issues of *Hustler*.

Elvis Peebles
SUNY, Duluth

What a charming concept, prufrockery. So how do I presume to employ it? Shall I say we? No. I should let you tell me. I am sorry for writing this. I must be better organized when I sit down to correspond, really.

unsigned
Harvard University

This may have as little to do with your etymological method as the method itself has to do with the genetic engineering of peas, but it was my grandfather, Cletis William Crow, who in 1952 along Chesapeake Bay trapped and sold to local markets a crustacean he called the Prufrock Crab. He contended that it was a rare subspecies of the delicious Maryland blue crab. Eliot does allude to the odd locomotion of crabs in his dreary, ridiculous monologue, but I doubt that my grandfather ever read a poem in his entire, salty life unless it was penciled above a public urinal. My now deceased granddad claimed to have named this crustacean subspecies himself, although I never knew why or how he came up with *Prufrock*. On my last visit to the Chesapeake shore, in 1991, I did not hear the term *Prufrock Crab* down at the docks, nor did I see it on a menu. Perhaps the creature has gone the way of the dodo, as we all will.

L. Wilbanks Crow
University of North Carolina, Chapel Hill

Honestly, Schrapnel. These deranged explorations and coinage fiascos you call a scholarly column are beginning to dampen my appetite for the exponents of academia. How can you sleep at night? Or on the more melodramatic side of inquiry, where do you sleep at night?

George
Quebec

WEENIE ROASTS AND ECOTAGE

It was the queasiest of times. I sat in my urologist's waiting room reading a back issue of *Outside* magazine, their fifteenth anniversary model. It was my annual checkup, that probe of the southern hemisphere that will wet the eyes of even the darkest Green Beret. I scrutinated blurbs of environmentalists' comments on the high points and low points of their movement over the past fifteen years. For Yvon Chouinard, founder of Patagonia, Inc., the zenith was learning from a newspaper survey that 85 percent of Americans call themselves environmentalists.

"One problem, though," he goes on, "is that environmental groups are made up of a bunch of weenies—of scientific types and gentle thinking people. They're not real doers, and those are the guys we need. This isn't the time for education; it's time for propaganda. This isn't the time for mild civil disobedience; it's time for revolution."

Amen, mon frère, but *weenies?*

The etymological evolution of *weenie* in slang, as Mr. Chouinard no doubt employs it, is oddish. Rawson notes that before the eighteenth century, *weeny* designated something small. Around 1844 it was synonymous for small child. And after 1929 it referred to a girl or a girlish man. In modern student slang, from at least 1950, a *weenie* is one of those threatened subspecies of industrious students who make their peers look bad—a dweeb, perhaps, or pencil geek or study bunny. Weenies are often descended from bookworms by birth; and *weenie bin* is the carrel wherein a dweeb lights to study.

In *The American Heritage Dictionary,* third edition, however, the slang call on *weenie* is "a person, especially a man, who is regarded as being ineffectual." Chapman's slang volume defines *weenie* similarly, suggesting *jerk* for a synonym. *Ineffectual* is the key and common word in each definition, meaning "not producing, or not able to produce, the desired effect; inefficient; weak; as in ineffectual remedy" (*Everywhere*).

Weenies? I had to know.

So a few days after my urology encounter, I asked an old university acquaintance, now immersed in the environmental movement to the tips of the stubble of his shaved head, if he thought Chouinard's evaluation was fair and soothfast. Since my old friend requires anonymity, I will refer to him as Forrest Jones. Forrest Jones calls himself a master of ecotage. He is a saboteur, dedicated to the prevention of the corporate rape of the American environment. He travels about this violated Republic spiking trees, springing traps, cutting and smashing fences, ripping up survey stakes and generally monkeywrenching any and all forms of machinery aiding in land development. His heroes are Genghis Khan, Robin Hood, and Hurricane Andrew. He is a bit of a misanthrope, and I am certain that he is a secretly sanguinary fellow on occasion.

Recently Jones was in Sarasota and Manatee counties, Florida, collecting names and addresses of county commissioners and various local politicians. I did not ask him why. We met at a beachfront restaurant on Anna Maria Island, where I read to him my etymological work in progress on *weenie*.

He grinned and said, " 'Ineffectual' is good, yes, quite accurate. Most environmental organizations are a crock of wormy fools who get off watching itsy-bitsy birds, or identifying pukey-colored butterflies, while the habitat near and around them goes down at a more methodical and embarrassing rate every year, sort of like your Buffalo Bills at the Super Bowl. And all that these meek and creepy little environmentalists do is wring their pale, skinny hands and turn the other cheek. Oh, sometimes in a periodical cicada swarm one might write a concerned letter to his or her crooked, criminal congressman, or some other slime-cake politician who's on the secret payroll of big industry and rampant development at any cost. But mostly, you do have huddles of weenies out there. And that's why a few of us must be at war, Schrapnel. You own a gun?"

Forrest Jones's zeal is something. You have to be charmed, to say nothing of alarmed, by his outlook. I wish him well and pray that he is never captured.

But of all places, it is in contemporary American poetry that *weenie* first arises in the disparaging sense in which Yvon Chouinard uses it. And here is the quatrain by Anne Tichborne-Blackadder that appears in the 1979 edition of *New American Women Poets with Bugs in Their Buns* (Freebase & Son).

MY LOVE ON FIRE

'Tis not my day for kiss or toast.
I'll not go to your weenie roast,
Nor let you in to gawk my scenery,
Since you, yourself, are such a weenie.

It is indeed the proverbial small world. For it was Anne Tichborne-Blackadder who was accomplice, or rather sidekick, to Forrest Jones on numerous ecotage outings into Vermont ski country during the mid-1970s. Forrest relates that Anne had to retire from ecotage in 1977 and pursue poesie full time when an antipersonnel mine accidentally detonated and removed a portion of her left foot. Already a bitter and suspicious woman because of the sudden homosexuality of her estranged husband in 1972, Anne became increasingly negative toward things that even hinted of patriarchal dominance.

But strangely, Forrest Jones's last news of Ms. Tichborne-Blackadder came in the form of a snip from the loony column of a New York City daily, circa 1984. She had been arrested, it was reported, at a New England resort for tossing slit bags of road salt from a moving ski lift.

"It was very weird and sad," Jones recalls. "The last thing she said to me when she was in the hospital for foot surgery was that the radical toe of the environmental movement was, quote, 'a bullshit masculine gimmick, a vain variation on dragon slaying.' I don't understand her anymore. Why, I couldn't even get her to dump sugar into a bulldozer fuel tank, and then she goes and gets pinched for bombing slopes. She sure chucked her weenieosity."

There are more traditional aspects of *weenie* upon which one may teeter. There is weenie as frankfurter, that staple of American sporting events, family picnics, and toga parties. And alas/alack, there are the sexual overtones and undercurrents of the word. But if you are a regular peruser of this column, you have already entertained such tangents unconsciously, I'll wager. You may even wonder why I've not veered toward some penial discourse in conclusion. Don't ask.

Chronic prostatitis is not easy to hide or cure. But I am glad to see that you are finally resisting those lopsided tirades on the sexual that punctuate your early columns. Do come visit us at the clinic if you do not improve. We are experimenting with a new battery of antibiotic treatments that so far are producing rejuvenating results. It's too bad urology was not so advanced in Thomas Hardy's day.

P. S. Grandstaff, M.D., F.A.C.S.

We here are offended by the way you ignored the most American of weenies in said column. May you choke on your next hors d'oeuvre. May someone slip a drop of lysergic acid in your next cocktail. May you dry up and crack.

Oscar Meyer
U.S.A.

Anne Tichborne-Blackadder wrote that her use of weenie was a slur reflecting on size and prowess of her husband. She did not wish to suggest that he was an ineffectual jerk. You are the jerk. You can look it up in the 1981 collection *Feminist Epistolary: The Poetess on Poesie and Valium.* It's in one of Anne's letters in there. You really are a male chauvinist warthog.

Hazel Lufkowitz
Dallas, Tex.

POONTANG REVISITED

The epistolary tradition is not an ideal arena for verbal joust; that is, the letter is a cheap and cowardly medium for attack, correction, suggestion, or rebuttal. But since this is a syndicated column, you bet I will not pass over and ignore the outrage and malignment spewed my way recently by one Elvis Peebles of (so he boasts) SUNY, Duluth. In questioning my etymological analysis of *poontang,* Mr. Peebles blurts that the word appears onomatopoeically in an unpublished short story by Ernest Hemingway entitled "Nick and the Carrot Stick." OK. Furthermore, he declares that Hemingway's use of the word "predates all that you [I] claim in your [my] column, quagmire cranium!"

I am here to tell you, term termites, that Elvis Peebles is mostly full of radiator sludge. First, to reiterate, my reference to the theory that *poontang* is a bastardization of Philippine is verified in Eric Partridge's seminal slang dictionary. Robert Claiborne places the word's English debut at circa 1900, which is twenty-seven years before the hand-dated manuscript of the aforementioned Hemingway piece. This fact was illegally faxed to me by my younger sister in Boston. Her doctoral dissertation concerns Hemingway's unpublished short stories and the motif of the transvestite as a trickster archetype. She is an up-and-coming authority on Papa, despite her Newtonian Feminist Deconstruction orientation. Now, admittedly I did not include dates in my original *poontang* essay. But must I spoon-feed every juggins that can read?

In addition, the passage that Mr. Peebles insists boguses my explanation is (as far as sanity can determine) erroneously construed by Elvis of Duluth on at least one point. The text goes:

Ricky aimed the Daisy at the rusty pot still and closed one eye and squeezed the trigger bravely.

"Poon-tang!"

The lead .180 BB hit the empty pot this time. It was the Spring of the middle of the war and Ricky was a brave and clean young man who was sometimes dirty. Toby smiled at his sun-burned nephew.

"Poon-tang!"

It was a good BB gun.

Hence Mr. Peebles's analysis that Hemingway employs *poontang* onomatopoeically or, as Peebles writes, "to denote the sound he hears when Toby Atwater's nephew shoots his pneumatic BB gun at the empty pot still." Fine. Onomatopoeically? Yes. But pneumatic? No. Mr. Peebles's ignorance of the technical history of the BB gun is shameful and nerdish. Hemingway of course was familiar with the ballistics and dynamics of this American tradition. For the lead .180 shot was used by the Daisy Manufacturing Company, Inc., until 1930, when it was superseded by the .175 steel shot. No doubt the small weapon Hem refers to is the Daisy pump model no. 25, which was made from 1914 to 1978. This was not a pneumatic gun, however, as Peebles assumes, but a spring air gun. Daisy introduced its pneumatic line in 1972. Hemingway was dead.

As for the BB gun historically, well, it is an American institution that began in 1886 when the Markham Manufacturing Company of Plymouth, Michigan, introduced a wooden gun called the "Chicago," which fired a size BB shot. On January 16, 1889, the Plymouth Iron Windmill Company, which bought out Markham, developed a similar metal gun and was granted sales rights. Daisy is the offspring company. Daisy moved to its present home in Rogers, Arkansas, in 1958. Just ask Mr. Orin Ribar of Daisy's customer service department. He is a knowledgeable and friendly ambassador of a great American company that has touched millions of boys in this century during their various rites of passage.

With that revealed, let us hope that Elvis Peebles and cranks like him will do a little more thorough research of their own before accusing any columnist of perfunctory scholarship. It is no doubt ill-educated mentalities like that of Peebles who are responsible for the muck of alarming newsprint nationwide now questioning the safety and sanctity of the BB gun. Headlines like "How Safe Are BB Guns?" or "Boy 10 Blinds Hippopotamus with Grandfather's BB Gun!"—all of which sing with unfounded hysteria about the sale and use of such low-powered target weapons—are yet another example of the hissing false tongue of the media, the real snake in the grass (what's left of it) of our straight-shooting Republic.

So, like the pen or the typewriter, the BB gun is only as true as the hand that guides it. Education is the key. Read Grits Gresham's article in the April 1991 *Sports Afield,* "How to Hit an Aspirin with a BB." It contains salubrious instruction for the insipid myriad who cannot swallow pills whole and must powder or fragment their oral medicine. You know, like your cousin the vegetarian president of MADD. Or your thirty-year-old neighbor, Willard, the block captain who pedals his twenty-four-speed mountain bike a mile to the local library every Saturday morning to do volunteer work in the science fiction video corner.

Gawd!

Turn on the country radio station in the morning and listen to Earl Pitts! Or learn to play the single-reed harmonica, a Hohner, just like Jimmy Fadden of the Nitty Gritty Dirt Band. Mommas, don't let your babies grow up to be Elvis!

Good grief.

And never dismiss the slime upon the fig leaves in Cleopatra's Basket. It got there somehow.

In Thomas McGuane's latest novel, *Nothing But Blue Skies,* you may read the following: "There was something about the way she touched her fingertips to the droplets of resin on the pine bark that made Frank think, *I may be headed for a world of poontang.*" Who says contemporary novelists are mostly a bunch of smut mongers? Why, there are at least a dozen more offensive words besides poontang that McGuane could have used in that context. And at least three of them begin with the letter P.

L. Fiedler
at large

I applaud your attack on Elvis Peebles. He was my literature professor fifteen years ago at Notre Dame. He was dismissed for his eccentric classroom stunts done in the name of audiovisual aids—like dragging a cadaver around the room while trying to lecture on Poe and releasing a live garter snake before reading Dickinson's "A narrow fellow in the Grass." He is a lunatic, and he carries a pearl-handled derringer, I was told.

Gwen
Detroit

PRESAGE IN THE LAST POEMS OF TOULOUSE MARS

(While this essay was not among Adventures in Etymology *but originally appeared in a now obtuse literary journal published in northern Florida in 1992, an awareness of Dr. Schrapnel's first study of Toulouse Mars is helpful if you long to understand those Adventures that do deal with Mars, two of which are included in this collection.)*

Deconstruction be screwed! Give us bio crit or give us death, as certainly the stormy life of Toulouse Mars blazons. That this Cajun proctologist turned blank verse prophet was not the accordion-tugging, piranha-grin womanizer and happy camper that many critics claim ought to be so many deli cuts over the scales by now. Mars's upcoming and posthumous *Rat Hole Serenade* (Fecund & Sons) gurgles with foreshadowings of his recent and swampy seppuku. Here in the blithering nude are those creepy semaphores that can only be construed as absolutely foggy autobiography, dark plans, slithery snips of forecast and threats that must be assessed as brash and Plathian prognostication for sure.

"But the mother is dead!" railed his former bobsled teammate Lance Luanamoa to probing Fecund editors. "What the Hades you want my frigging letters for? You knows my bloody bio will be done soon and to be definitive, suckers. Don't you try to bogart me in the name of your frigging back-biting scholarship, toads!"

Such a quaint response to the memory of Toulouse Mars is common, particularly from those who were close to him for the mere six to nine months that he was known to endure any relationship outside of his immediate family. Hence his nickname—

Shorty. It was unusual, then, for Toulouse and Lance to correspond for over a decade; and unique it was that Mars persuaded Random House to publish Luanamoa's debut tome of spooky children's verse, *Crumb Snatchers Beware.*

Sadly, though, the stout Polynesian was too late in repaying the debt; it was he who suggested the title *Rat Hole Serenade,* lifted from an unrecorded song by balmy Shreveport blues legend Garfish Cohen, who once weathered a bayou fortnight with Mars when they were commissioned to collaborate on the score for Peckinpah's since abandoned cinema adaption of *Sir Gawain and the Green Knight.* According to Luanamoa's text, the rhum-riddled sessions took place at a shack in a remote and wet cranny of Louisiana that was owned by a late cousin of "de Garfish," as Toulouse called him. Guitarist Cohen blindfolded Mars and rowed him to and from the clandestine studio in the family canoe. The tapes are said to be "misplaced," in the lingo of Garfish Cohen's former recording company, Turquoise-Azure.

But if *Ariel* is truly the most outstretched suicide note in recent literary history, then the dribble of poems that comprises *Rat Hole Serenade* is the curtest of swan songs. It is indeed a troubled outcry, wherein we can finally see which twentieth-century bards most severely influenced Mars, how modern philosophy rattled his willy-nilly spiritual dislocation—New Wave Calvinism—and which contemporary periodicals Mars most wished would print more of his work. Thus *RHS* is a horrendous and drained contrast to the frolicking Toulouse Mars of *Glee, Sissy, and Me; Me Squeeze-Box, Yes!* and the erotico-romantic epic, *Donald and May Mooning at the Bay,* volumes that Chicago critic F. Knox Elgin reluctantly cheers as "some of the schmaltziest shit you will ever read."

Two key poems in *RHS* could have been perused by, say, Mars's friend and Freudian astrologer Billings Fontana, and the whole messy suicide might have been prevented or delayed. Perpend the following oddity, written one week prior to that fatal and overpublicized hike into central West Virginia's Cranesville Swamp, where Mars faced his Whatever by throwing himself between two rutting, twelve-point bucks, following his usual "roughing-it" lunch of two bottles of Guinness and a Moon Pie.

Existentialism Begins in (city)＿＿＿＿＿＿＿
(state)＿＿＿＿＿＿＿＿＿(zip)＿＿＿＿
wormwood!
the gods are just
silly
what do
the chartreuse vikings
know?

your pants!
look at your pants!

First and too obvious is the title's allusion to a short poem by
James Wright (yet another dead poet), a piece that Mars knows
and describes in his precocious M.A. thesis as "mill-hunk hermeneutics." But slivers of that blue-collar gloom, grandly reminiscent
of the Ohio-born Wright, dot much of Mars's terminal book of
verse. Here are those lines from his only political piece, "Reagan,
You Pagan," an economic, middle-class lament that is certain to
be uttered by the Democrats despite the refusal of the *National
Review* to print it as a cover inlay on a November issue. Take this:

you keep old neighbors Rockefeller rich
to snore in the big house with that mouthy wench

ain't life a gleaming crescent wrench?
    and poor ole Smith
  gassing in Wendy's parking lot
his American Dream in your hands becomes Scheme

Oompah! Oompah! decries the tuba

A valid digression indeed, but does not the use of fill-in-the-
blanks in Mars's existential title continue the motifs of rootless
wonder, detachment, and early Alzheimer's that machinegun the
pages of *RHS*? Linking the political and the philosophical here

are the Vikings and the Pagans, a technique so true to the Marsian panorama, dazzling as Sartre and Camus in the funhouse. But the diction of the full poem under heed above blares, in the patois of Mars's waxing technician and adjunct lover Bonita Derailleur, "Gonna keel myself!" Consider the imagery, as subtle as a Stegosaurus in a card shop. Wormwood. Now, who else but a poet? There is the rough parody of Edgar in *Lear.* Notice the one lone and sickening color that must surely render vanquished any heroic import associated with those Norse rakes. For the overwhelming question that accompanies the constant Vikings knows in itself how far epistemology may jog. We all know.

Finally, there are the ominous trousers, a recurring frustration in Toulouse Mars. Recall his 1989 commemorative sestina, "Sturm und Drang de Levi en Carpe Diem Baby," where he groans of his being overlooked, yea, shunned, as the archetypal protagonist for the Dockers television commercials. It is a poem that oddly bleeds and steams with all the poignancy of those media ads, as evocative as a pair of beige slacks in the reference stacks.

But it is the near inextricable cant "Letters to the Editor," the three-part poem found in Mars's vest pocket—and stained with the poet's very lifeblood—that the vers librist's gnawing distresses puke forth in near primal heaves and contractions. And while the old, lusty Toulouse seems to want to bust out in the poem's opening stanzas, spiritual ennui prevails. Nature is crass. His women are all golfers here, and not, say, "those poetry licking broads" of his early limerick series, "There was a young lady from Haiti." The author here wrestles with change and rejection and fumes about what he might do. The poet, he surmises, must tell, tell, tell his fellow poets. And it is as if poem suddenly metamorphoses into letter bomb. One imagines the frazzled poet charging the small window near the rear of the pharmacy and insisting on priority mail, that the deed will proceed with uttermost velocity.

LETTERS TO THE EDITOR

I

I want virgins! not poets!

I crack tortilla chips! not tears!
Tears are for poets!

Yo the spring grass sucks
at my red jogging shoes
and the sun blossom sputters
like a woman
golfer.

So by now you wonder
where is this all
going?

It is going
to the *American Poetry Review.*

II

APR you obfuscation
squat on my heart
and you will not
get my Ezra

pound limericks
extraterrestrial cows

I am
Director of the Writing Program
at Anal Roberts University.
You are next!

III

You are so pubic
yes pubic!
Like the swans
yes swans.

Might it be the herpes?
Perchance the music?
Oh i cannot remember.

Dear *American Poetry Review*
my subscription
has run out.

So while "I" of Letters hints of energy and intent, "II" threatens and struts. The artist's ego mushrooms and flaunts, and there is a dash of chagrin there that the aforementioned light verse was not acknowledged by Legman in his classic collection of the limerick. Note also the veiled identification with the persecuted poet, E.L.P., and the Fascist baggage implied. Thus in desperation the poet tries self-deification, the old don't-mess-with-me-because-I-run-the-show trick; I administer the creative writers; I know more than you do, and it is a religious institution, editors, folks, or "creepers on tacky bark," as Mars once called a pair of gay Los Angeles reviewers who referred to his *Squeezebox* collection as "fodder of such stinking magnitude that the mind's nose cannot imagine, so long as marijuana and LSD remain illegal."

Nowhere in Mars, then, are the urbane influences of both cummings and McKuen more disguised, the mythos of poet and periodical more frontally attacked. Modern institutionalized spirituality, evangelism, the very foundations of metaphysical perversion and normally clothed body cavities—are all fingered. But it is all an obscene, if you will, gesture in miscarriage, as we are dropped into the superbly catholic "III" subtitled "za charm" in an early manuscript draft dated 14 October 91 and discovered stuffed into the cigarette lighter socket of Mars's noxious Volvo by a bank officer (more fuel, perhaps, for Professor Wellington Heebs's theory that Mars was a closet environmentalist).

For there is thorough resignation in this third "letter," an almost pastoral blitheness toward the final knowledge that a retreat into fundamentals, back to basics, even an old-fashioned flop in the weeds—all of those warm and traditional possibilities sung by and for the poet—are dead. It is too late for anything, save suicide, because there is the incurable, the Malady. And whether literally rampant, or psychologically conjured (or both), it Zambonis the crimson-spattered ice of the Oversoul. It hoovers the stench-laced paisley rug that warms the Subjective Superlative—dichotomously the heart of poetic inspiration and the hormonal seat of bodily joy. It cleans you, then makes you cold.

Thus the poet shudders into the lower case *i*, to make way for that closing and haunting couplet that is at once plan and premonition, rhyme and reason, as well as the sprightly ironical inscription on Toulouse Mars's grandiose tombstone. End marks, after all, were the only punctuation that Mars employed in *Rat Hole Serenade*. So it is fitting that his own period follows him to his grave.

But somehow, someone should have known, because galleys or drafts of all *RHS* poems were in the hands of editors and critics prior to Cranesville Swamp. Unfortunately we live in a critical age where *friend* hints of *fiend*, when meaning is topsy-turvied in the name of analytical criticism. If the current critical milieu was one worked by men and women giving hoots about honest sense, one poet might yet live. Those literary demolitionists who opt instead to wave the pennants of nihilism and iconoclasm as they charge into the critical foray must wake up and smell the blood to help.

Deconstruction be screwed, and Toulouse Mars, R.I.P.

MARTIAN WARPS AND KLINGON PROVERBS

No contemporary person of letters displays the supposed proclivity for mixing, salting, and assaulting English, and its drove of conservative themes, like the late Toulouse Mars. Nor have any recent writers poemed effectively in extraterrestrial, nonearthbound languages in the manner of the erratic Cajun doctor of rectal distresses. Perhaps it is this irregular comixture of the softly iconoclastic and the gothic intergalactic that makes Mars's best work appear inaccessible to so many of today's literary critics. Ironically, the fact that most poetry reviewers are anal retentive is surely another reason why Mars goes so unheeded critically and is poopooed at best. Of course there are the biographical interpretations accorded his posthumous *Rat Hole Serenade,* wherein the depressed poet cries for help and gets none. So he commits a bizarre suicide in reality. But his self-slaughter gained him the same sort of misguided, one-sided critical attention that stomped about the grave and books of Sylvia Plath for decades. It is worm-hole analysis.

A more anfractuous and preponderant aesthetic challenge is Mars's obscure chapbook *Wanda the Warp,* printed in 1983, somewhere betwixt the publications of the unmitigated ham of *Glee, Sissy, and Me* and the romantic, riotous drivel of *Me Squeeze-Box, Yes!* There are experiments with language, linguistic risks, in *Wanda the Warp* that make *Finnegans Wake* read like *Jonathan Livingston Seagull.* Now, I know that there are tribes of archetypal critics in Indiana who insist that *Finnegans Wake* is *Jonathan Livingston Seagull,* and vice versa; but this argument is best resolved by Anthony Burgess or the weenies at the Audubon Society.

The key word and motif in Mars's odd chapbook (it is but thirteen pages long) is *warp*. He employs the word almost exclusively as a noun throughout the armpitful of poems therein, and therein looms a peculiar yet protoplastic equivocation heretofore overlooked by scholars and readers at all familiar with *Wanda the Warp*. Thus the piece (*work*, if you will) represents a preeminent philosophical shot from Mars's booming canon, recalling a spiritual specter that the poet had to face repeatedly and stare down, only to see it finally reappear in the form of a twelve-point buck, whereon Toulouse became a bloody, tattered hood ornament, if you will.

Shakespeare wrote: "Though the waters warp, / Thy sting is not so sharp / As friend remember'd not" (*As You Like It*, II, vii). *Warp* here is synonymous with freeze. And in Thomas Gray's "The Bard" (1757), we find: "Weave the warp, and weave the woof, / The winding-sheet of Edward's race." *Warp* in this case is a noun, denoting the threads that run lengthwise in a woven fabric. So much for poetic tradition, and its failure to beam light on the thesis here. Toulouse Mars would have loved this paragraph.

Nowadays, when warp is used as a noun, it refers to the state of being twisted or bent out of shape—a distortion or a twist, especially in wood. There is more. But for now, when warp is applied to a humanoid, the arrow is innuendo. One who is a warp has "a twisted or distorted disposition; an aberrant personality; a misfit; a Yale sophomore" (from *The Princeton Underground Slang*, 1985).

Ergo, Dr. Harvey Rightmule, the renowned Navajo Deconstructionist, observes that *Wanda the Warp* "chronicles the poet's alarming, self-destructive, and not-so-secret lust for a crazy, smelly bayou bitch with crooked bicuspids." Rightmule bases his overview on a couplet found at the bottom of page three (*trois*) of the chapbook: "Wanda, though thou art the warp of the bayou, / Jiminy, baby, I has to love you!"

Warpy Wanda, as she is tagged in a later sonnet, is seen as a femme fatale, then. She is Mars's Cleopatra, with snakes dripping from her like Medusa in season, to paraphrase Dr. Rightmule. "The poet cannot help but succumb, despite his cognizance that closeness is trouble in nearly every aspect. For she is all too tantalizing, like the hiss of the shiny serpent," says Doc Harv.

Really, even the most tenderfoot herpetologist has to guffaw at Rightmule's simile. Very few snakes actually hiss. And the critic who sees only the dark side of the warp misses the ying/yang essence of *Wanda the Warp,* ignores the equivocative vitality and subtropical ambivalence that saturate Toulouse Mars's chapbook. Moreover, Wanda represents the double-edged bread knife of her poet. There is, then, a sharper side.

To see this aspect, one must look to additional definitions of warp, such as: (v.) to move a vessel by hauling on a line that is fastened to or around a piling, anchor, or pier. Warp (n.) is also a towline used in warping a vessel. This nautical undercurrent is certainly something Mars, an ex–Coast Guard officer, would not have overlooked. Furthermore, since we know that he owned videotapes of every *Star Trek* episode through 1990, including those Next Generation installments that smack of Lewis Carroll (Charles Lutwidge Dodgson) forever attached intravenously to a bottomless liter of chilled hallucinogens, the intergalactic/extraterrestrial motif suggested earlier is an in-character leap here.

Look it, Trekkies and multidisciplinarians! We all recall that warp factor 1 is the speed of light; and that warp factor 2, 3, and 4 (etcetera) are geometrical functions of light velocity. MPH is warp factor cubed. And the maximum safe speed for a Constellation Class starship is warp 6, although the *Enterprise* once attained warp 14.1 when its matter/antimatter integrator controls became fused, prompting Scotty to don his kilts over his head. You can look it up in *The Star Trek Concordance* (Ballantine, 1976).

Toulouse Mars knew his warps. And he knew how to weave the constant and cosmic fables that veer through *Star Trek* into a poetics with no metaphysical peer in this century. His apologue, and its frenzied genius, is asseverated by the chapbook's unnerving epigram, which is an old Klingon proverb:

qaStaHvIS wa' ram loS	Four thousand throats
SaD Hugh SlijlaH	may be cut in one night
qetbogh loD	by a running man.

Here is the poet out of control, dangerous; and he knows it. But he is also aware that his amuck must be checked and/or surfeited.

He senses that Wanda the Warp is the nostrum for his deleterious disposition. The chapbook discloses the process of such a realization, which is at once and also an Initiation. Such a journey/ordeal is more than hinted at by the opening poem.

> *bang/ghargh*
> I am a running man.
> Who can sate my razor?
> He says, "Seek the Warp
> Or you shall just get crazier."
> And so, Warp Wanda, *galegh vIneH*.

Toulouse Mars's awareness of the ambivalence and ambiguity of his quest is revealed by the title of this poem; *bang* is Klingon for one who is loved, and *ghargh* is a serpent or worm. He intuits the duality of his desideratum—the warp, Wanda. On one side, there she is in all of her antisocial glory (*ghargh*), and on the other (*bang*) she represents the karmic towline that fastens the poet's wavering spirit to land, security, society, safety, sanity, Platonism. In another sense too, Wanda is a time warp because she can suspend the poet almost simultaneously in seemingly opposed worlds, two places at once almost. Mars desires to know and experience both; *galegh vIneH* translates "I must see you."

Midpoint in this slight book, the poet seeks counsel from Cyril, the swamp shaman, who tells him, "Wanda is a warp." Mars asks in Klingon—*Duj shosTaH nuq*—"What is coming toward the ship?" Actually it is his canoe. Cyril shouts back, "Do not shun her foamy warpitude!" And the poet inquires further—*nuqDaq 'oH Qe' QaQ'e'*—"Where is a good restaurant?" Thus Toulouse Mars accepts the gnaw in the belly of his soul and knows that it means business. He will take Wanda out to eat for starters. He realizes that he requires spiritual sustenance and warp companionship, the sort that only the flip/flop idiosyncrasies of Wanda the Warp can fulfill. That is, he probably will not get laid, but at least he will not starve. And that helps. For in Cajun folklore, warps are forever celibate creatures, with baccalaureate degrees in Culinary Arts;

but they love to glaze themselves and their companions in crayfish oil and wallow the night away. That is important.

The chapbook's final verse brings peruser and poet the proverbial full circle and is reminiscent of Campbell's monomyth.

LOINS AND BRAINS
Geezy me, taken hovel with a warp!
Let it be; I stash my blades on the wharf.
Don't I know it, and have to crow it!
Warpspeed to you all. Go home, and don't blow it.

On a note of the trumped carnal and the oversexed spiritual, *Wanda the Warp* concludes. Finally the searching poet has accepted totally the necessity of such a marriage, as suggested by the allusion to a Beatles song and the reference to the hero leaving his knives behind. That is to say, the cross-training of the penis is no longer paramount. And there is a kind of joyous relief at this dephallusment, symbolic though it is. The poet will sing of his journey/lesson, just as the Ancient Mariner was obliged to, or as Marlow is compelled to after messing with Kurtz.

Warp, then, is not always a derogatory noun, although the transcendental (anchoring) associations probably are not intended by a statement such as "Fluffy is the biggest warp I know." For more on the conversational slang dynamics of *warp*, track down Dr. Paul Kruty in the Art and Architecture Department at the University of Illinois; or look up his brother Peter Kruty, a New York artist and book designer. Either can tell you more.

And for additional Klingon, try *The Klingon Dictionary*, by Marc Okrand. There is a language, a language that looks and sounds suspiciously like Germanic Russian, with a hint of those ancient rock carvings I once saw in the remote mountains of West Virginia. But I suspect that there are some glorious war poems in the Klingon literary tradition, verses that make "The Death of the Ball Turret Gunner" sound like Ogden Nash on the courtship of crickets.

While you are correct to point out that very few snakes actually hiss, thus causing you to cachinnate at Dr. Harvey Rightmule's analysis, it is likely that Toulouse Mars was familiar with the eastern hognose snake, which hisses loudly when disturbed. *Heterodon platyrhinos* is common in Louisiana and all of the American Gulf coast states. This nonpoisonous reptile will also spread its neck skin like a cobra to discourage aggressors. If this tactic doesn't work, it will roll over and play dead, mouth open and tongue hanging out—another fitting metaphor for critics like you.

Dr. C. W. Krebslichen
Dept. of Herpetology, LSU

In reference to a couple of your columns of last spring, did it ever occur to you that J. Alfred Prufrock is a weenie? Or that he is a closet warp? If so, call me and we can have lunch and talk the next time you are up here to spy on William Safire.

Amanda Ruth Peters
Washington, D.C.

Warp this, you charlatan. I scarcely know how to dispute your thinly veiled contention that the late (thank the gods) demented Toulouse Mars is a major American poet, tragically snuffed out in his debauchery-laced prime. Then again, I'm not sure such literary lunacy deserves rebuttal. One cannot expect an archetypal warp like you to understand or appreciate the truly fine poets still alive who continue to elevate our literature, which cannot be yours too. Name one, can you?

N. Phelps Boone
Eugene, Ore.

Your readers should know that Warpsylvania Press will release an anthology of Klingon war poems in December. The book is entitled *Vaporize Them All!* and is a bilingual edition. The Klingon Empire is mildly grateful for your attention to our tongue as it is ineptly used by your wormy writers. Nevertheless, not one *yoq* will be spared when our fleet arrives to cleanse your planet.

Captain Kor
Battlecruiser Kothos

WHAT TO BUY YOUR WORDMONGER

Often I receive letters from readers who wonder what gift book to give to their favorite etymologist in the family, neighborhood, or wherever. It is not so easy and obvious as one might suspect, because the traditional day of the Wordmonger—Wordmongermas—according to the Nargoomisiad Etymological Calendar is May first. May Day! May Day! Thus most of us who work on the word origins and evolution front are reluctant to accept presents of professional content on the usual occasions of bestowing, like Christmas or other birthdays.

Case in proverbial point is Rudyard D. X. Thatchwingle, Etymology Chair at the University of Dwelbs, who, one Yuletide morn, heaved his new *Compact Oxford English Dictionary* into the fireplace and shouted to his wife, "Dumpling! Never give me occupational gifts on any day but May Day! There are ancient laws!"

Indeed, it is eccentric. And it took three months of weekly visits to the chiropractor to relieve Dr. Thatchwingle's spinal trauma, a condition common in etymologists who think they can flip the *OED* about like so much pocket dictionary. Nearly as ominous are the various species of unabridged word books out there. "Them's some heavy mothers," I once heard a young graduate assistant exclaim. For sure, a session with the mother of all dictionaries, and/or her offspring, can hurt you if you insist on machismo, cavalier handling of these cumbersome volumes. And contrary to lexicographic legend, women are not impressed by such feigned ease of juggling. So wear a back brace under your tweed.

Now, as May Day approaches, here is a random selection of books for that special etymologist. Not all of them are reference works, because even a word archaeologist has to read a story once in a while, even a poem. Thus I assume that the working wordmonger already owns the core texts and such—the *OED* and a handful of slang and origins dictionaries—or at least has easy access to them. Next comes the branching out, the wetting of the feet, and the eventual immersion. Ooo! And always keep one eye on *A Dictionary of American Regional English.* And don't ask how come.

A complete concordance to Shakespeare (usually the Bartlett one) will enable the etymologist to salt his/her eventual writing with fashion and class. Truly outrageous are the possibilities, since Shakespeare said so much and used so many words; and the Bard is the apical appeal to verbal authority. Do not go out to buy a new concordance, however. I purchased mine from a former student (Lois Schneider) for twenty-five cents. And that student bought it for a dime off of the sale clearance table of a small, rural branch library in New Martinsville, West Virginia. It is a 1937 edition, but you know the Bard. He has not written a word lately. In addition, I am told that William F. Scarlet's supplement to the concordance is forthcoming, inexpensive, and perhaps nearly worthless.

Fiction should not be overlooked when you are shopping for your etymologist. Be advised that *A Clockwork Orange* is an amusing, though conservative, favorite. Undergraduates still spew out research papers on Burgess's use of Nadsat, the futurist street slang of Alex and his droogs. But if noxious sedatives are your bent, there is *The Bridges of Madison County* (still) and its author's relapse, *Slow Waltz in Cedar Bend.* Too bad if you missed the Book of the Month Club's offer last autumn to purchase both "volumes" at once for a ridiculously reduced price, still a rip-off. And too bad the Soviets no longer have an ICBM targeted for Camp Hill, Pennsylvania. But "author" R. J. Waller has now "created" two middle-aged, existentialist, romantic, quasi-environmentalist shithead "heroes" whose wavering brains are yet slaves to their shrinking testicles. It is to snore, unless you are a young American novelist trying to penetrate the literary scene (if there be such a niche today) of U.S. publishing. Then it is to weep and gnash.

Silly Sayings from Billary and Hill is a new book by the noted D. C. humorist and political commentator P. U. O'Shames. Reviews so far indicate that the author may not have acquired his two hundred pages of aphorisms by bugging the White House, as his preface maintains. In fact, his sibling rival, F. U. O'Shames, recently told Larry King that these "warmed-over Poor Richardisms" are the hastily edited texts from three years of taped phone conversations between the author's aged grandmother and senile great aunt, recorded somewhere in the Ozark Mountains. F. U. may be right. For it is hard to envision the First Lady snapping to Al Gore, "Hey, a tree's a tree / When you got to take a pee." Nevertheless, encounters with deceit and dirty birdcages can sharpen you.

For pure and focused scholarship, it is always a trick or treat to peruse the ongoing work of Maxwell Marshton Hopps, Ph.D. This Cambridge lexicographer, now eighty-six years old and still writing, has added to his canon a two-hundred-page monograph on the word *show* that is at once telling and shocking, as thorough a piece of research as you will ever find to challenge the trendy journalists' attitudes that the products of the university presses today are, to be sure, pedantic and pretentious, to a degree that even a well-educated reading audience struggles, if you will, to extract the rich meaning and analysis that is so very often the sparkling hallmark of venerable and experienced academics the world over, whose syntax and diction—to say nothing of their philosophic and philologic grace and stamina—are the remaining fortresses in the never-ending war on the forces of the popular presses and their cliché worldview, seen once through rose-colored glasses but now eyed through the bottom of empty brown pharmaceutical bottles.

In addition on the recent critical waves there is the unbelievably unforgettable gem, blurbed in an October 1993 *Publisher's Weekly,* as follows: "*Blood, Bread, and Roses: How Menstruation Created the World.* Grahn, Judy. Beacon Pr (Farrar, Straus & Giroux). ISBN 0-8070-7504-3. Nov. Cloth $22.00. The feminist author of *Another Mother Tongue* offers a mythographic study of the interconnections among ancient menstrual rites and the development of agriculture, mathematics, writing, calendars and other realms of knowledge."

Undisclosed sources abed with the publisher tell me that the sequel to this book extends the author's thesis to include chimney sweeps, CD ROMs, the English sonnet, and the Loch Ness monster. Holy tampon, folks. Like deconstruction (Deconstruction), and the New Americanist field of literary criticism, Feminism is a bottomless urn of multicultural ash, hard and soft nihilism with an axe to grind, Renaissance man neutered and singing. And you see how it can inflict a rattled tone upon a usually vaudevillian prose temper. Worst of all, Judy Grahn is a very good poet, whose rags-to-riches autobiography may be delayed now in favor of another tome for the walls of the Feminist manifesto.

Finally there emerges a poet on the international scene whose experimental verse, and language, is a kind of spiritual enema to etymologists trained on the wonders of the *OED, DAE, FBI*, etc. He is E. Talbot Donnywhissel, a former Zulu tribesman educated at Slippery Rock University in western Pennsylvania, M.F.A. from Iowa, and a doctoral candidate in nuclear medicine at Johns Hopkins. His initial chapbook, *Listen to the Scorn,* is a sophomoric tribute to an unmentionable early influence. But it is in his second volume of verse, *When Men Were Men and the Flocks a'Skittish,* that Donnywhissel develops that unusual blend of African dialects and Iowa redneck slang that so baffles and delights the critics. This odd linguistic idiosyncrasy, coupled with the theme of bestiality on a cosmic scale (a direct reversal of one of W. B. Yeats's queerest motifs) is what makes E. Talbot Donnywhissel, in one reviewer's view, "at least as important to world letters as the Marquis de Sade, Richard Poe, and Euell Gibbons."

Most of these works are available at quality and quaint bookstores. So there.

NOSING AN OBSCURE TROPE

Chicago, home to at least one of America's most obdurately conservative universities, has always been a smelly place. For *Chicagou,* according to one Webster, is Algonquian for "place of the wild onion." But some scholars dispute this meaning of the Indian name and offer *skunk,* or *powerful,* as English equivalents. But screw the scholars. Chicago was so named by native Americans for the horrendous number of wild leeks (*Allium tricocum*) that once grew there. *Ramps* we call them today, from Illinois through Pennsylvania, down to the Carolinas and up to southern Quebec, the northernmost range of this powerfully pungent perennial with leaves like those of the lily, edible bulbs like wild onions, and an odor reminiscent of the stench of a thousand dead condors rotting in southern California sunshine or the truffle trove near Dordogne.

In rural West Virginia it is against the rules to eat ramps in school or to attend spring classes with ramps on your breath or elsewhere. You see, ramps in addition have a giant, penetrating smell that lingers and malingers. Pervading they are. Their chemistry permeates your entire being, so that when you eat ramps, then sweat, their great odor leaks onto your skin via your perspiration. Aah, fabrication this is not!

And the wild leek is a vegetable rich in folk and mythic tradition. Ramps thrive under the sign of Aries (March 21–April 21). Thus it is conjected that *ramps* is a modern shortening of Ram's Son. But before you anticipate wrongly, a connection between ramps as capillaries of the interstate highway system and the snappy plant is doubtful; for these leeks do not grow near the on/off ramps like so much chicory but are found in hardwood forests during early spring. Usually the first and greenest shoots of the forest floor, they will grow straight through a late snow, unbruised, probably thanks to the astronomical acidic content of their stalks and leaves. It is a high-test ascorbic acid, vitamin C, that makes ramps a valuable spring tonic and the object of many fine ramp festivals throughout Appalachian mountain communities in April, yes, yet the cruelest month.

The taste of ramps resembles a mixture of onion, garlic, pepper, and my Uncle Quail's stale beer mustard. But ramps are an attractive botanical, although the smell can render some folks comatose. Ramps can ruin a party, unless all guests partake, since a fix of ramps is your only defense against the irrefragable presence of a lone leek nosher. To confound and stir ambivalence, ramps are reputed to be aphrodisiacal, which can make for orgies. The Marquis de Sade, recent scholarship shows, ate the European bear leek (*Allium ursinum*) by the bushel. Sigmund Freud favored this continental cousin to the American ramp also, as did D. H. Lawrence and Djuna Barnes. So if menstruation is responsible for agriculture, math, and writing, as poetess Judy Grahn contends, is it so preposterous to credit the wild leek for erotica and its subspecies?

Aah, but incredibly, what this all heralds is another chapter in the volcanic life of that Cajun proctologist versifier the late Toulouse Mars. Mars's notebooks are due out (Crockmeir Press) in late 1996, and among the surprises in this possibly dubious collection is a facsimile of the only villanelle Toulouse Mars ever wrote. Leroy X. Fontleroy, editor of this yet untitled volume, supposes that Mars wrote the poem following his attendance at a ramp festival in extreme rural West Virginia, Helvetia exactly, in 1979. Helvetia is an old farming and cheese community settled generations ago by Swiss immigrants. The most elderly Helvetians retain their Germanic accents, a refreshing contrast to the southern, hoopie twang of their neighbors and young descendants educated in mountain schools. Or is it?

In Mars's poem "Acquainted with the Ramps," the real and surreal aura of *Allium tricocum* is glimpsed in all of its mythic and putrid demeanor. Additional motifs are that of social bonding, where the poet sees the ramp festival as a kind of Appalachian Canterbury Tales event, attracting annually "my friends abroad of various stamps." And of course Toulouse Mars is keen not to shun political and electrical commentary when, in stanza 4, he alludes to the annoying fact that the town of Helvetia has (in 1979) but two streetlights.

But most dominant is the divine sense of ritual here, the knowledge that the ones who partake of the seasonal dinner of ramps, and everything, acquire a heightened sense of spirit that transcends their physical torment and olfactory apocalypse. Ramps are realized as a recharging agent for the soul's batteries. And even in his deep-rooted Cajun crawfish stew of a brain, Toulouse Mars knows the universal semaphore in the ramp and its festival, and then some.

Thus let us begin our exit with Toulouse Mars's ramp poem:

ACQUAINTED WITH THE RAMPS

I have been one acquainted with the ramps,
Driving out in rain, and back without fright.
Although my entrails rage, my spirit does not cramp.

'Though my whole body burns, I gleam like a champ.
There is no doubt. I have eaten the light,
And now I am one acquainted with the ramps.

Certain, too, my conscience will never damp,
'Though my breath be putrid, my pants a sight.
So what if the entrails rage? The spirit shuns the cramps!

And what if the Helvetians can afford but two lamps?
One seeks a primal odor, neither wrong nor right,
Once one has been acquainted with the ramps.

Then yearly make the trek to the mystic mountain camp.

The cure be taken, anoint impending blight
And let your entrails rage. Your spirit will not cramp.

Thus you, my friends abroad of various stamps,
Rest assured the myriad stench reflects a chastened height.
For we have been, indeed, acquainted with the ramps.
Let our entrails rage. Our spirits shall not cramp.

Forsooth the poem stinks, to be sure; but there is the rub. What Toulouse also attempts and achieves here is a pure and simple exercise in that little-known Neo-Classical trope *malodora-poeia,* or the formation or use of words that imitate the smells and rancid rhythms of the objects to which they refer. You won't find that one in your Holman/Harmon, English majors. So stick with the renegade prof if you are seeking a truly virgin dissertation topic. You don't have to make literature so accessible.

Talk about stink! Why, I remember a few years back when some editor of some West Virginia magazine put ramp juice in the ink for his spring issue and sent it all over the country smellin' up post offices and homes and newsstands and bookstores everywhere. And don'tcha know the feds just give him a reprimand and made him promise to never do it again. Now, I ain't gonna make no jokes about how your stuff stinks without the ramp ink, cause I do like your columns sometimes and was almost a English major once myself til I realized I could make more money and raise a family better by workin' in the mines.

Orville Clintwood
Salem, W.Va.

Richwood, W.Va., is home to the momma of all ramp feeds. "Feast of the Ramson" began there in 1917, and there you can sample ramps in a variety of wonderful recipes—cooked, stewed, etc.—or you can have your ramps raw, the way of the true mountain gourmet. Some of us even eat the leaves.

Blanche Griffin
Juneau, Alaska

We in the etymology community prefer that you resist your cheap imitations of the late Euell Gibbons and try to concentrate on word origins about which scholars might give a good goddamn. Ramps, Schrapnel? Really, I doubt that even Toulouse Mars would find your column on the wild leek enlightening. Furthermore, realize that the leek is the national emblem of Wales, probably because legend declares that one who wears it in battle will emerge victorious and unscathed. You steer a leaky boat sometimes.

Jonathan W. Waite
Yonkers, N.Y.

If you will meet me in Helvetia on the last Saturday in April, we can attend the ramp festival, toast Toulouse Mars, and bury the hatchet. I have mellowed and have forgiven you since your *bop* column embarrassed me a year ago, and I no longer wish to kill you. In addition, I have an idea for a paper on Peruvian aphrodisiacs that requires your sincere edification, participation, and advice.

Clyde

 SCHRAPNEL'S LIST

Words come and words go, it seems. When a word, phrase, or idiom falls into disusage, when it gets old and is seldom said, it is called an archaism. Employment of an archaism garners a *Dx* (diction error) in writing classes—developmental, expository, or creative—or will drop eyebrows to low tide when echoed in conversational English. Aah, yes, snobs will be snobs, we used to whisper during those grad student mixers once a year at the home of the chairman of the Department of Linguistics. Oh, snotty youth. Thus "Words will be words" has become Schrapnel's First Law of Usage (SFLU). I know. The acronym looks like something signifying a new university in Florida; but remember, scoffers, that the English alphabet contains but about two dozen useful letters.

But this thing about some words, and their declining usage, is something deserving arrest on almost a yearly schedule, perhaps requiring annual review. Therefore, I give you the first installment of "Schrapnel's List," or a six-pack of words we should not lose to archaism syndrome, a contagious affliction spread by teachers and reporters (and a few students) in our 28,800 bps age of contemporary vocabulary bashing. So here are some good words that ought to be kept afloat in the language gumbo for generations, no matter what journalists and English profs say or write. Use them and see.

1. *Bogart* is a verb from the name of the deceased film star, Humphrey Bogart, known for his rough roles. To bogart, according to Chapman's slang dictionary, is to behave truculently, or to get something by intimidation. It can also mean to take more than your share, and was especially current in the late sixties and early seventies druggie talk, as in, "You bogart that reefer again and I'll

. . . oh, wow, man . . . cool!" Perhaps the most recent (April 1, 1994) use of *bogart* (also *bogard*) dribbled from the lips of TV intellectual Rush Limbaugh when he attacked President Clinton's health care proposal: "Ya know, Slick Willie is jest gonna hafta learn that you can't bogard the American people inta not bein' sick."

2. In the third stanza of *The Rime of the Ancient Mariner,* Coleridge writes:

> He holds him with his skinny hand,
> "There was a ship," quoth he.
> "Hold off! Unhand me, graybeard loon!"
> Eftsoons his hand dropped he.

Eftsoons, from the Middle English *eftsone* and Old English *eftsona,* means "presently" or "at once." It is an archaic adverb with an eerie drone to it. The Calusa Indians used to say that when the cabbage palms shout "eftsoons," the storm will soon be upon you. The *OED* notes, however, that, "The notion of 'soon,' though app. implied in the etymology, is not directly evidenced in early examples, and down to the 17th C. is sometimes absent; but in mod. archaistic use the sense is commonly 'forthwith, immediately.' " So use *eftsoons* the way it sounds and not to denote "by and by." Just take our words for it.

3. It was Paul Simon and cohort who recorded "The Fifty-ninth Street Bridge Song," a musical piece of 1966 that is often poorly compared in sophomore introduction to literature courses with Wordsworth's famous Westminster sonnet on a similar structure. The hook of the song is "feelin' groovy." *Groovy,* as jive talk, actually predates Simon's tune by about thirty years. *Excellent, wonderful,* and *far-out* are synonyms for groovy, one of the sappiest, yet catchiest, modifiers to move into and fall out of Hippie Kulchur. Then there is *groove* as noun, which denotes an intensely gratifying activity or something exciting and desirable. As a verb, *groove* can mean "to like and/or approve" or "to perform very well." "Groove on! Groove on!" is the battle cry of Sammy the Satyr in F. Farnsworth Rumple's 1968 erotic epic *A Thousand and*

One Grooves, which a Deconstructionist at Yale lately interprets as "an agnostic celebratory and extension of those eighteenth-century nuances and neomotifs of subtext that have bedeviled the critical tempers of readers of agro-micro Western texts from the days of Laurence Sterne down to the very decade of Masters and Johnson." Nevertheless, let us retain and use with pleasure *groovy* and all of its kin.

4. At last year's Schrapnel family picnic and spelling bee, I heard one of my K-age nephews spout the word *flogrobbin* (FLOgrobbin), and I had to ask.

"I don't know what it means," he answered. "I just thought to say it."

Since my nephew is really too young to remember Dan Quayle, I assumed his reply was not some sort of parroting paraphrase. After further inquiry and jelly-bean bribes, the post–rug rat confessed, "Aah, Uncle ——, I just made it up. I never heard it before."

"Well, do you think you can use it in a sentence?"

"Aah, you got any Reese's Pieces?"

No matter. *Flogrobbin* has possibility in this age of light-speed hip and hogwash. So let us find a context and denotation for the word. Remember that the first and accented syllable is *flo* (long *o*) and not *flog;* otherwise an association with physical punishment may be made. *Flogrobbin,* then, cannot mean to deprive a sadist of joy. And if used as a noun, *flogrobbin* (note the double *b*) cannot be the redbreast who beats his fellow birds with a worm. Pronounce the darn thing correctly first, then figure the meaning. Then send this department a nice letter.

5. "Dear Shitferbrains" is a favorite salutation of radical environmentalists, particularly those who write letters to the *Earth First! Journal.* "Dear Shitfer" and "Dear SFB" are affectionate short forms. The traditional slang import of the idiom *shit-for-brains* is thoroughly pejorative, denoting a very stupid person. Earth Firsters have taken that edge off of the phrase and have even streamlined it. TV intellectual Rush Limbaugh receives many letters with such a greeting, but not enough. In addition, one might imagine President Clinton himself getting salutations from

hard-core environmentalist that go, "Dear Shitferbrains, Your plan to build 5 billion dollars worth of roads in America is the most UNGREEN thing a man could do, since most of those highways can only lead to further destruction of Mother Nature."

So let us not lose sight of "shitferbrains" in our everyday speech and reconnaissance. It is assuredly a barbed phrase, among other things, but needs attention and gainful employment. After all, colleges can't do it all.

6. Finally, if the adverb *basically* disappears from English without a similarly easy synonym to replace it, millions of college-educated people will not be able to start a sentence. *Basically,* you see, is basic to introducing any variety of thoughts:

Basically, what you're saying then . . .
Basically, I just don't think . . .
Well, basically, it's . . . [*Well* here is a verbal pause]
Basically, Penelope . . .
Basically, you . . .
Basically, what they . . .

Got the picture, baccalaureate toters?

Now you know, readers, Schrapnel's List 1994. But the real credibility test for the list, some will argue and jab, is whether all six words can be used in a snappy sentence that reflects or refutes the contemporary milieu. To that I say "pig bath." Anyone can write a trick sentence. And "Adventures in Etymology" is no muckraker journalist's corner wherein, under cover of pop scholarship, some smart-ass language maven takes his proverbial cute and cheap shots at the Clinton administration. You see?

Sentence shmentence, Adventures buffs. I want to see some sestinas! You know, that old poetic form from Europe that utilizes six end words instead of rhyme. Look it up in Holman and Harmon's *A Handbook to Literature.* And don't overlook that tricky envoy. This time there will be some great prizes, donated by the MLA Itself and the Academy of American Poets (if the Academy has a good grant-writing return this year). So send me your sestinas now!

dear sfb ... you done it. ... you become the perfect sloth when you call for your readers to send in definitions for words you can't figure ... when you ask for pomes in an outdated mode that only the most mega-ancient of creative writing profs would assign. ... you let me down. ... you don't say nothin' no more. ... gonna go out to drink the primo mescal til the worm devours my soul.

frostbite freddy
the village

Who appointed you vocabulary monarch? The words that you suggest are necessary are absurd and archaic already. They're dead, deadbeat, except for that preschool drivel that you try to pass off as charming. But if you're getting into neononsense now, check out David Grambs's *Dimboxes, Epopts, and Other Quidams* (Workman, 1986), a collection of ad hominems more pretentious and stupid than any of your Adventures.

Celeste B. Harmon
Burpers Bend, Colo.

Groovy is not in danger of becoming an archaism. Its currency in journalese is high. I did a database search on my computer yesterday and found over thirty instances of the word *groovy* in headlines and quotes over the past year. Why don't you buy a computer, cheapskate, so you don't make such erroneous assumptions? Do you think William Safire looks all of his things up in an old library? Get with the close of the century, Schrapmon.

Marley Gates
Kingston, Jamaica

Basically, your column is not the groovy piece of flogrobbin you eftsoons bogart it to be, shitferbrains.

Wally the Weed
lost in Idaho

Your column is the reason I am canceling my subscriptions to *Popular Linguistics* and the *Journal of Degenerate Aesthetics.* Damn syndication, anyway. You and your ideas are too iconoclastic; and like Gore Vidal, you should change your name.

W. Peter Brandocks III
Barrow, Alaska

Bravo on your Schrapnel's List! If the *New Yorker* and the *Gettysburg Review* carried a column as witty and satiric as yours, I might still subscribe to them. But alas, mediocrity is too much with us, and I fear that another Pearl Harbor is just over the next wave.

Ogden Whitewater, Editor
Cool Hemlock Review
Helvetia, W.Va.

# CLOTHING THE GAP

The much-celebrated director of the Environmental Library in Sarasota County, Florida, Linda R. Backer, B.A., M.A., M.L.S., showed me recently a list of headlines five pages long from several major sunshine state newspapers. The gist is this: Man Dons a T-Back to Peddle Hot Dogs; T-Back-Clad Vendor Faces Sex Charges; Hillsborough May Narrow T-Back Ban; To T or not to T, That Is the Protest; City Council Members Want T-Back Ban; Thonged Vendors Get Legal Stare; Dispute Suits Bathers to a T; Cleavage Issue Wearing Thin; Sarasota Rewrites Anti-Nudity Ordinance; Religious Group Calls for T-Back Ban.

Ms. Backer was not researching options for her summer wardrobe but had just completed a computer search for a local merchant who owns a swimsuit shop and was supposed to appear on a national TV talk show with three of his models who had been arrested for wearing their scrimpy t-backs at public beaches. This purveyor of minute bathing attire, one Pierre McTwatch, apparently desired to get current on all of the state and national publicity (pro and con) covering this latest polemic on nineties beach propriety. He did not return to the Environmental Library, however, to claim or pay for his data search. And Sarasota County slides deeper into debt because of its border war on prurience. For in addition, county commissioners hired some heavy-hitting consultants from Salem, Massachusetts, to rewrite their antinudity law; and P. McTwatch owes the library system twenty-four bucks.

Aah, t-back. Yes. The furor in Florida is a royal hoot. But the thong bottom is scarcely new apparel anywhere. Shakespeare alludes to such a garment in *Timon of Athens* (IV, iii) after Timon bolts to the primeval forest in sudden poverty, where he denudes, and denounces humanity and all of its creature comforts in a way not unlike the ravings of Lear on the heath, or Andrew Dice Clay on his chemicals. Timon's mad, misanthropic near nakedness is described to Telephone by Alcibiades thus:

> Forsooth and a phooey! See he aback
> In rhyme like a naked tree, back?
> Ye see him with his arse adrift?
> See how he wears it like a naked tree, back!

A. C. Bradley contends that this odd, seemingly nonsensical construction "tree, back!" is as close as the Bard dared come to the then taboo name of the scandalous thong, without challenging the Globe censors. And it is G. Wilson Knight who reports that Alcibiades' lines above drew the heartiest of roars from the ground goofs, a laugh-level rivaled only by some of Mercutio's gutter talk in *Romeo and Juliet* and perhaps a line one act later in Timon that is shouted by the beleaguered Eucalyptes after one of the commissioned harlots bites his knee: "Oh, I am lame!"

Yes, the t-back (*t* is for thong) may seem new and alarming to the great jumble of retired Puritans on coastal Florida, but it is old hat to literature and literary figures. Recent biography reveals that the Brontës wore thong bottoms under their flannel nightgowns. But the most famous t-back anecdote occurs in an out-of-print collection of rare letters between F. Scott Fitzgerald and Marianna Demoliccia, a third cousin to Matisse, who once told Scott that *Tender Is the Night* "reads like Milton in ten-foot seas."

In a letter simply dated March 13, Fitzgerald recalls that he wore one of Zelda's undergarments over his eyes while playing Pin the Tail on the Poetaster at one of their New Year's Eve parties, the one that raged well into February from Paris to Zurich. Scott writes:

> Zelda's scanty t-back is, I must confess and reveal now,
> as you are of the blood of an artistic family, the reason

that I won the game. For there was not enough of it to tie around my head to effect a wholly suitable blindfold. The guests were simply too tight to notice that I and I alone could peek at the enormous derrière of Gertrude hovering over Alice, and thus was able easily to drive soundly the antique fountain pen (a gift from Picasso) squarely center of either cheek. It is, I must admit now, a repulsive and disgusting memory. But I can yet remember how wonderfully smooth and soft the silky t-back felt on my bare ears.

Yes, the relationship of the thong, t-back, g-string, et al. with literature and burlesque is a long one. But I wondered why one— to beef up on ongoing data, opinions, laws, incidents, prices, arrests, whatever—would choose to conduct research at an environmental library, a facility for scientific fact-finding. Undoubtedly Pierre McTwatch was fishing for reasons, appeals to authority, facts, clues, or cute remarks that might help him keep the t-back legal, popular, and controversial. He is an American.

So I returned to the Environmental Library a week later to investigate for any practicable connection between the bare buns phenomenon and Mother Nature, as the Romantics might accent Her. Chance did indeed crack me across the chops, as my brother the outdoor writer says, for the very first browse volume I slid from the stacks suggested a link. It was in the book *Ecological Determinism and the Demise of the Textile Industry,* by Willow Lynn Ginn, that I read the following:

Thus the impending global warming may be a blessing because the Earth's animals and natural resources are disappearing at such a shocking pace that sometime around the middle of the next century the raw materials and cuddlies used for most types of clothing will no longer exist. Extinction creeps across the face of the Earth for so many species, like angleworms in the driveway after a hard rain. And what clothing might be available in the future, like coats and jackets, will cost so much that only the highest of Republicans will be able to afford it. Cotton will be as scarce as lice on a Tylenol caplet. A severe apparel shortage will be upon us by the year 2051. Good it is that the planet gets warmer. (872)

If Ms. Ginn is right, then all of the blazing fuss over the donning of t-back swimsuits at beaches and weenie wagons smacks as more than a tad silly. For in the future we will all be forced to wear less and less clothing, more abbreviated garments, for reasons of climate and supply. Why not get accustomed to it now? Stop complaining, gawking, slobbering, hyperventilating, etc., what all! Only fools reject the inevitable. This time it appears that good old-fashioned family values and disorganized religion are out to lunch with Dan Quayle and the likes.

It was my longtime spiritual consultant Father Dementio who declared often in the country club spa that if God's children were meant to possess an abundance of body coverings, they should have been born with some. "What do you think Adam and Eve wore to the beach?" he often asked with a grin, followed by a slug from his jug of special wine. The good padre had a point, I suppose. Similarly, one of the most ignored laws of logomachy (if that front can be said truly to have laws) is that usage is a bare and slippery thing. So the Adventures do not stop just because.

It is no surprise that a perverted, Godless pig like you favors public nudity, the very kind the t-back swimsuit advertises. Isn't it true that your doctoral dissertation is entitled "The Marquis de Sade and Hugh Hefner: A Comparative Study"?

T. Baker
Austin, Tex.

As president of the American Federation of Swimsuit Makers,
Local 1069, I would like to thank you on behalf of my union
membership for your support of the thong swimwear. America
has been held hostage by conservatives for too long. And it is
getting hotter out at the beach.

Spike Mason
Brunswick, Ga.

We at Kelly Girls have a way to render "t-back" in typewrit-
erese. You use a close parentheses first, then capital T, then
open parentheses. Also, you can backspace/halfspace twice for
a tighter fit, like this:)T(or)t(. Also, you can raise the T as
you might for a footnote number and get a higher ride, that is,
if your machine has a carriage scroll release. Or you can just
say t-back. Maybe we will see you at beach volleyball. I wear
a neon green one.

Taffy Thomas
Pensacola, Fla.

ROMANTICISM NOW AND THEN

I. THE SNOBLEM OF DEFINITION

Surely believing himself vogue to the gills, Senator Cartwright Quentin Grubb (R- Tex.) blurted to a horde of buzzing journalists outside a new Austin steakhouse, "This heah Clinton administration, now I'll tell y'all, they want the American people to swallow this big, green pill they used to call romanticism, or maybe some kind a THOReau enema. But I say us Texans ain't in the market. I mean, sure, the environment is important, 'cause that's where we take our oil from and other things. But those other things come first. Like Dan Quayle and George Bush tried to tell y'all. So y'all can jest take that an' your recycled notebook paper and use'm where the sun don't shine!"

Even the most skilled disciple of Deconstruction may be taxed to dejumble and discover something ratiocinative in Senator Grubb's metaphoric and grammatical miasma here or there. Adding to his verbal logjam is the politician's perception of enema dynamics, clearly in a state of reverse polarity at best. That may explain why so many high-ranking Republicans feel the way they do. That's polbiz, though.

Next day headlines for this intellectual and near-literary encounter declared, "Senator Blasts Clinton's Romanticism."

Gadzooks! *Romanticism* . . . and away we go once more. Now there's a word or three—*Romanticism, romance, romantic.* Common agreement on a definition of *Romanticism*, particularly among writers and artists (to say nothing of scholars and intellectuals) has been—according to A. O. Lovejoy—one of the longtime, ongoing scandalous exercises of literary theory.

Indeedy. For at least two hundred years the literary mastiff and its fleas have grappled with *romanticism (Romanticism)* and its oft confused and misused variants, *romance* and *romantic.* Most of us know that *romance* does not always denote a love story when we use the term in a literary context. The popular Harlequin drivel that is pumped out by a thousand authors a year and is read by millions of people and such is not quite romance as it was pursued by Nathaniel Hawthorne. Nor is a romantic necessarily one who reads love stories all day and most of the night and owns a dozen sets of bed sheets of various nontraditional fabrics (leather, silk, rubber, glazed cotton, ribbed polyester, burlap, or recycled encyclopedia pages). I once knew a lusty, nerd M.B.A. candidate who glued back issues of *Business Weekly* to her mattress. Majors not of the liberal arts get their jollies in the damnedest of ways. But even writers who should know better don't have much of a clue as to what Romanticism truly entails (or curtails), where *It* has been, or where *It* is going today. Here is the scoop.

Any dictionary, be it Websterish or specialized, begins by noting that *Romanticism* is an artistic and intellectual (don't worry) movement that originated in late eighteenth-century Europe. Wouldn't you just know it. Principal characteristics of Romanticism are: a heightened, zealous (often religious) interest in nature (Nature); balmy reverence for the individual's right to express his/her emotions and imagination, no matter how weird; a departure from and spitting upon the tight forms of Classicism (fear not); and a rebellion against established social rules and conventions, no matter how cool or seasoned.

Romanticism, then, is bound to be revolutionary and raucous, yet the Romantic is one who worships Mother Nature or at least exhibits respect (sometimes awe) for the landscape. You can add that the Big R is an "anything goes" attitude injected heterogeneously with egalitarianism, environmentalism, individualism, transcendentalism (Romanticism's complex American clone, sometimes disparaged by the British as "Emerson's Enema"), and tempered nihilism. None of this extended definition is terribly definitive, but one could gather that, just as one may gather ye rosebuds.

So you see, we can land on a generally sweeping definition with which most readers will sleep. But there will always be (trust) a scholar or twelve somewhere, quick to finger a flaw, a gap, an exception or oversimplification, contradiction, a lack of specificity, or a mislead. Fret not. For this is what a scholar lives to do. He blows the general breath one wheeze closer to specific halitosis. He turns us one screw thread deeper into the power line next to the stud behind the library wall, where hang those portraits of Thomas Dewey and James Billington. And you know what happens when the turn of the screw pierces the insulation—the lights go out. The moonlighting prof is knocked on his ass. We have sudden nonsense and the old ignorant armies crashing into the night trick. Don't we? And how about those metaphors?

Romanticism is many things, forsooth. But it is predominantly an immature, nature-boy sentimentality, a silly and naive outlook on the nature of things, quite non-Lucretian, as it were. But by God, it is impressive when flaunted properly, and it still helps a lot of poetasters and homespun philosophers to acquire much casual coition. You see, women love it because it does have, when postured well, a dash of hot sexuality to it. Today's and yesterday's roguish Romantic—often bearded, dungareed, and raving—makes things happen. He/she does effect juices.

Historical case in point is that blazing Briton versifier George Gordon, Lord Byron. Scholars and walk-in clinics report that Byron copulated with more than four hundred females, not all of them *Homo sapiens*. What could be more thoroughly Romantic? It is a track record that yet defines and glosses all concepts of Romanticism and has done as much for the public image of poets as the off-court exploits of Wilt Chamberlain have achieved for the legends of the National Basketball Association.

The celebration of the individual spirit is the second most important Romantic particularity. The Romantic asserts his/her unique character with unabashed zeal and emotion, and thus the Romantic is often regarded as eccentric. The Romantic may be a loner/recluse (cf. Emily Dickinson sometimes), except when a bunch of them get together to lie down to block a logging road. At such times you have a bevy of Transcendentalists flirting with a felony. Civil disobedience, then, is the Romantic way of righting perceived wrongs. And because human life is unquestionably precious (hogwash!), no one gets killed (cf. Thoreau or Gandhi). To some realists, however, Romanticism is a quite worthless political tool, especially when the issue/clash is hard-core serious, major moral, global, and archetypal. Look: war is war. And large, efficient weapons (not gargantuan, slobbering mouths) most often generate a win (cf. Nagasaki or Hiroshima). Money helps too. But since penury is a flashy prerequisite to a Romanticism honor badge, well, you know.

Forrest Jones, the undercover ecowarrior extraordinaire whose philosophy and deeds make Earth First! look like the Campfire Girls, observes that in a political or social protest you can spot the Romantics quickly. They are the ones whom the police or military carry off by their limbs. "Because when it's confrontation time," Forrest says, "Romantics just go limp like a hognose snake. In the throes of their CDS (Civil Disobedience Syndrome) they become so much human pasta on the arms of the law—a little messy, but easily removed. Just a sloppy, temporary inconvenience that has no bail money."

And while the underground Forrest Jones reveres the natural beauty of this nation planet, diminishing as it is, you do not dare call him a romanticist (don't ever call anyone that). Neither is he a radical environmentalist, as so many Romantics think they are today. You know, those aging hippies and reformed drug addicts still trying to push their post-Woodstock whackoisms down the throat of a doomed society sick with greed and ignorance. Forrest Jones is a killer, I fear, who will assassinate some key perpetrators of what he calls the Snuff the Planet Mentality (land developers, politicians, the Husseins of the world, and their like lawyers) before he meets our Maker himself, on his own terms.

"My going," Jones once told me with an eerie and sagacious grin, "will be a glorious one of my own calculation, I promise you."

II. PERVERSION WAVES ITS OILY DOOFUS

One cannot avoid returning briefly to Lord Byron here, easily the most singular personage in all of Romanticism. His influence does not end with the wowing of his peers and post peers but spills into other corners of the art world as well. Particularly, it was Byron's play *Sardanapalus* that influenced Delacroix's most showy exponent of Romantic painting, *Death of Sardanapalus,* a work whose exotic and frolicking images, along with its appalling violence, holds enormous appeal for the Romantic mind-set. And it made a Methodist of my Uncle Freeman. Sardanapalus was the raunchy-rich Assyrian king who, when surrounded by attacking enemies, removed to the innermost room of his palace and had the whole joint (gold, silver, royal wardrobe, baubles, etc.) set afire. He shut his concubines, eunuchs, horses, etc. in the room with him and ordered his guards to slay them before the impending cremation so as to avoid the discomfort of certain and fiery death (What a guy!). "In the midst of the carnage," writes art historian Tom Prideaux, "the King lies on his royal bed, oblivious of the massacre he has commanded, in a state of total renunciation, perceiving the futility of trying to fight off his enemies, forswearing the world in all its beauty, all its delights, all its strife."

On the other appendage, *Death of Sardanapalus,* with all of its nudes and knives and blood trickling down the elephant's brow . . . good grief, to some it's just another sadistic orgy. But for some reason, the image of a disillusioned Great One gathering about him all of his treasures and murdering and torching them just to piss off the world closing in on him, well, that's romantic (Romantic). And as they say at the Missouri School—"Ya gotta see it ta baleev it."

This Sardanapalus sort of Romanticism (romanticism) is in part what informs the box office supernova *Jurassic Park* (sappy as it is), which has about as much in common with the novel of Michael Crichton as Bo and John Derek's Tarzan film with that first ape man story of Edgar Rice Burroughs. But no matter. Contemporary folks and writers, especially those involved in the popular modes of art and near art, and/or the media, appear bent to employ *Romanticism (romanticism)* and its variants every which way but literary anyway. As we were likely to shout in the pubs on a grad school Friday night, "A. O. Lovejoy is A-O-K!" And my grandfather's favorite expositional transitional expression was, "Looky heah!"

III. THE EXCELLENT FOPPERY OF THE PRESS

Etymologically, *romance* is a story written in the language of Rome (Latin). Specifically, *romance* came to refer to those medieval vernacular tales of chivalric adventure and knightly bravery and foolery (buggery). It is from this sense that modern definitions and variants evolved. From the 1730s to the present, *romantic* is associated with love, lovers, love affairs, and extremely suspicious friendships. And it was in the late seventeen and early 1800s that romanticism blossomed into the literary credo explained and ravished above.

But when you read *Romanticism, romance, romantic* in the newspapers and similar places, close contextual scrutiny is required if any exact meaning is to be salvaged from the term. Formalism is your handy tool. Even a good hunch will help. Then again, well, see for yourself.

A *New York Times* reviewer refers to the movies *Damage* and *Bram Stoker's Dracula* as romance, wherein the stories address the theme of romantic obsession. When I asked my widow neighbor, the lovely Gert Frothingslosh (Ph.D. in paleontology), about that assessment she said, "More specifically I would say those films are about erotic obsession, and actually, they both suck."

Rolling on, *Business Week* attributes much of the monetary success of *The Bridges of Madison County* to the novella's bright romantic vein; that is, there is a steamy farmhouse sex scene. (In truth, it's more gaseous than steamy.) "Here's a book," the reviewer further maintains, "that allows someone middle-aged to hold on to that kind of romanticism. . . . Maybe Madonna should take a lesson in subtlety." Maybe partly so. Last Thursday at Walden's I noticed a silvering couple checking out with copies of *Bridges, Sex,* and *The Story of O.* It was at a mall near Miami, and I thought I was lost.

But let us be fair with critics. For whether a reviewer of cinema or fiction, one's job is quite unreal, or surreal at best. Only an orthodox Romantic, or a transcendental optimist (on a very good day maybe the village idiot) can expect a critic working a deadline to be able to make consistently valid aesthetic observations and judgments. Reviewers don't have the necessary Gallo Option, which in vintage jargon translates as the credo about selling no wine before its time. And time and time only is the sole (soul) barometer of art. Reviewers do not have a lot of quality time to perform their work, so they compensate with yards of polished wisecracks and snotty ad hominems. As T. S. Eliot rants, "There is no more deluded, illinformed, insipid subspecies of the literary critic than the reviewer writing in the popular presses. To believe that one may read and judge, in a mere week's time or less, even a purported literary text, is pure bovine feces."

To stroke on, lifestyle reviews get no better if you are searching for *Romantic* in the old English class sense. A fashion feature in the March 24, 1993, *Fresno Bee* contains the following language effluvium: "The new spirit of bohemianism borrows equally from writer Ken Kesey and Nirvana's Kurt Cobain, blending early seventies hippie romanticism with deliberate no-style style of the Seattle grunge scene. And just like the music that inspired them, these clothes make a lot of noise. . . . Above all, fashion's new spirit of liberation is a symbol of change, an unmistakable denial of the sharp shoulders, short, tight skirts, and carefully matched pieces of the eighties power suit."

Such a description does smack of the rebellious stance of literary Romanticism toward Neo-Classicism. And Coleridge was at times a grunge. Similarly, the earthy odor of Thoreau was the topic of many good-Natured, fireside light verses at Brook Farm. But to suggest that the dress code of the MTV generation is partially striped with English and transcendentalist zoot suit bravado is scarcely camp or accurate.

Then there is the contention of a *New York Times* Sunday mag spirits column that, "Hemingway made rum respectable. Well, romantic, anyway. During his years in Cuba, he wrote all morning, then repaired to his favorite bar, the Floridita, for a potent restorative of lime juice, ice and good light rum." The writer here is surely romancing the comma. But try telling my ex-agent that rum is romantic in any sense. During my publisher's 1989 Guy Fawkes Party, she-agent drank three Zombies in fifty minutes, then retreated to our host's Porcelain Goddess for an hour of worship.

The next day she had contracted a bladder infection so rare, prolonged, and ferocious that the very suggestion of even the most rudimentary or remotest vaginal activity prompted her to contract and quiver like a hamster sprayed by a spitting cobra. That's how she tells it.

Lastly (suppress your amen), here is a headline and lead from the February 18, 1993 *Palm Beach Post:* "Commission Honors Artist's Romanticism: Artist Ty Wilson, famed for line drawings that feature romantic couples, received a Valentine's Day certificate from the Palm Beach County Board of County Commissioners thanking him for his 'dedication to a romantic and elegant bygone era,' as well as his contribution to 'the art world and Palm Beach County.' "

As for the prose here, it is to puke. And I don't suppose one has to see those drawings now to decide not to see them. And does not the latter quotation from the certificate have an oxymoronic ring to it? Furthermore, bet the ranch and the yacht that the Romanticism of the honored Mr. Wilson has as much in common with that of Delacroix as Thomas Hardy's moustache with Quaker Oats or Ecuador with the National Hockey League.

IV. THE DEATH OF EVERYTHING

Alas. Contemporary conceptions and usage of *Romanticism* etcetera are, to the followers of high art and literature, very distressing. Be advised sadly that this world is not a good and proper place wherein the traditional English and/or art history major may wave timeless denotative standards. For none other than the Supreme Language Maven himself (Himself), the Right Honorable William Safire, observes and declares, "After enough time, words come to mean what most people think they mean, not what we say they ought to mean."

When I made such a suggestion recently to Dr. Reginald C. T. Holyoke, Emeritus Professor of Aesthetics and Linguistics at the Saffir-Simpson College of Liberal Arts and Drama (Key West Campus), he inquired serenely, "Are you shitting me, Schrapnel? He said that?"

"Not I," said I.

"Oh, suffering succotash," sighed he. "Can you envision, then, the confusion that will arise in the literature classroom of future generations when our university-trained sons and daughters try to elucidate to the offspring of these libidinous unwashed, who crap up the campuses as we speak, that, say, 'I Wandered Lonely as a Cloud' is a testimony to the therapeutic qualities of Nature, ergo a cornerstone of Romantic thought?"

"No," I shot back. "But that does remind me of a passage in a novel written by one of my former creative writing students, a young man once incarcerated for undisclosed reasons."

I pulled the manuscript from my briefcase and went on. "The protagonist here is a disenchanted university professor, thirty-five years old, who resigns and moves to Siesta Key, Florida, to tend bar full time at a waterfront bistro of sorts. In this scene he flashes back to one of the last and most bizarre audiovisual presentations in one of his lit classes. Listen up, please."

From *Old Hitler; or, The Shark,* a Florida novel by Richmond Keys

Michael grinned. He recalled how he once preached of the Romantic poets' philosophical constipation, their infantile fascination with Nature, and their deification (try saying it fast) of the woods and fields and all of the cuddly brown animals who drink of the babbling brook, while their fine-feathered friends chirp formulas from verdant boughs (be sure you spell it right) above. It was the last time he tried some Wordsworth (which they weren't) and that thing "I Wandered Lonely as a Cloud."

He brought a bunch of daffodils to class in a tin bucket that had a quarter inch of charcoal lighter in the bottom of it. It was the cruelest month again.

"Now, as to this therapeutic quality of Nature to which the poet intimates; what say we expose his belief to the light of reason?"

He struck a wooden match on the desk and dropped it into the bucket. There came a fiery whoosh, and the yellow flowers wilted almost immediately, blackened and slumped like boiled spaghetti. Oh, the odor.

He read Robert Frost's "Come In," wherein the poet ponders the call of the Thrush at dusk, and whether the bird is issuing an enlightening invitation of some kind, asking the poet to enter the woods too and revel or something.

"But 'bullshit,' the poet says in the final quatrain. Listen again:

> But no, I was out for stars:
> I would not come in.
> I meant not even if asked,
> And I hadn't been.

"And Frost is right," Michael Davis McGill, Ph.D., concluded to his class. "Nature is process, decay, no darn fun. Frightening mostly. And it does not give a flying damn about little old you and your pain and suffering or the creep of your social disease. So be wary of the one who reads everything into Nature, because there is no creature so menacing as the orthodox believer, no cretin as dangerous and goosepimply as the disciple of misguided love. Be careful out there!"

McGill was never sure what he meant by that impromptu tirade, whether it was sage or symptom or both. Furthermore, as he strolled the warm, white beach now, westerly breeze through his hair, a magnificent frigate bird soaring above the green Gulf of Mexico so agleam with life—he was not so convinced of the folly of the Romantics. Not willing was he yet to secure the banner of William Wordsworth to his Fiero's antennae (Coleridge's maybe), but he could give the Romantics some credit finally. Gulfcoastal Florida felt too good to persevere in, at best, Agnosticism.

The emeritus professor smiled and lapsed into a stillness as easy as the very eye of the tropical storm. He sucked on his varnished corncob pipe, which had gone out but nevertheless smelled of the rich cherry blend tobacco that was his mephitic trademark. Then he uttered softly, as if phone ordering to Pizza Hut before the dinner onslaught, "I do trust that you failed the crazy bastard. Such perverse sacrilege and simplification must not go unpunished."

"He dropped the course, as I recall, and never returned for his folio. I was told that he joined the Peace Corps years ago." I slipped the manuscript pages back into a yellowed file folder and we both frowned.

"Hmm. Perhaps so, but by now he is probably a damned politician somewhere and one of those senators voting down pay increases for college professors and slashing higher education budgets."

"Not one of my ex-students," I assured him.

Dr. Holyoke scoffed, got up slowly, and trudged over to me, seated on his leather sofa. He sat down and put an arm around me and shook me gently.

"Ah, Schrapnel," he finally sighed, obviously moved to sadness. "We should have been a pair of ragged existentialists, scuttling across the floor of Sloppy Joe's."

You are a chauvinist warthog of the lowest order. Your suggestion that women are suckers for Romanticism, and will spread their legs for any poet/philosopher who flaunts it well . . . well! I had hoped that men like you became extinct following the Korean War. How naive I was, and how dismayed I am.

Margot Potts-Chambers
Charleston, S.C.

Perhaps I can clear up the idyllic and sexual tensions that rest upon your piece on Romanticism by pointing out that Romantic poems are not usually, nor overtly, snips of sexual verse, although they are often composed in the orgasmic mode. More times than not the poet gushes through and over some remarkable enlightening aspect of nature (Nature, if you will), as when P. B. Shelley ignores the bitch of a cold season ushered by the west wind and concludes: "If Winter *comes,* can Spring be far *behind?*" (italics mine). It does not take a terribly experienced Freudian analyst to see the latent sperm of those words, and given the implied sodomy of the thought, one must wonder how accurate it is to place Shelley in the Romantic mainstream with normal minds like that of Blake.

Dr. Axel P. Dogbain
Leeds, U.K.

you cranky crank! don'tcha know that those who write for the pop presses today gets their education at schools of journalism and teachers colleges that could care less about preserving your anachronistic literary definition of romanticism, which you so oddly lament is strapped to the heart attack machine? why do you think that today's high skool grads are so diddly? where have all the test scores gone, longtime passing? just awake and accept Bland Mediocrity as the new soul of our race, our future. . . . you can embrace the mundane just as easily as Whitman hugged the maple, so dig it, the Great God Bogus. . . . Him, baby!

frostbite freddy
the village

Congratulations, damned disciple of the ill read. Your analysis of Romanticism, in its attempt to pass as definitive, is merely sophomoric and deluded. It could set back literary theory several decades if believed by too many beginning students of literature. I am now a staunch advocate of censorship, and while I will not stoop yet to burning debase works in print, I would set on fire an author or two. I am not speaking irony here.

Begonia Prophet, Ph.D.
Smith College

I'll say one thing about your column. At least you don't harp on those minority things like gays and lesbians and illegal immigrants and AIDS and the holocaust. I'm a little tired of seeing story after story on such stuff of practically no concern to most Americans today. And what about those TV experts who say something like "The Flintstones" has no receding social values, and then they promote a group of teenage merchant turtles who use karate and smart-aleck remarks and still don't catch the criminal? Your story on Romanticism didn't make a darn bit of sense to me, and I've read most of the westerns anybody's ever wrote. But I'd rather read something that goes over my head than something that gets under my skin.

Frank Bob
Medicine Bend, Okla.

Eugène Delacroix cringed when he was called a Romantic, and your ill-informed example shows how little you know of art history. It is unfortunate that *Death of Sardanapalus* is too grand for a postage stamp, that you may lick it and better deal with its scope.

Jeanette Deneuve
Tacoma, Wash.

How dare you trash my all-time favorite flick JURASSIC PARK. You don't know what the hell your talking about, you bonehead critic or whatever you call yourself. JURASSIC PARK is a little romantic with those cute scenes with the kids and how the one scientist comes to like them and you know they're going to get married and have a family of their own. What could be more romantic than that. And I also like all of the Tarzan movies and will now look forward for the books to come out.

Jerry Riggs
Montgomery, Ala.

As usual, your idiotic Adventure omits key facts. While poets are always the first to call out for the protection of Nature, one cannot overlook the seminal contribution of Darwin to the continued substantiation of romantic philosophy. Does not *The Origin of Species* show that man is not a thing apart from Nature but a product of Nature? Of course, the Judaeo-Christian dogma and the Enlightenment have tried to teach us otherwise, and now look at the mess in which we wallow.

Dan Crow
Yellowstone National Park

GROUPERS AND SWORDFISH

Coleridge defines prose as words in their best order, and poetry as the best words in the best order. By implication, then, poems are a most demanding species of literary art, requiring from their diction a higher level of focus and discrimination than the language of story and essay. Ergo, the medium of poetry gives the beholder a more forceful aesthetic slap than syllables of prose. But the word choice of the poet is not everything. For there truly is only so much one can do with denotation and connotation. Music. A poet must feel the music of her words and know if that sound is right with the meaning. Objective correlative too, Eliot said of drama and such. Good poets select words and sounds that produce a system of appropriate imagery that rattles and arrests readers, illuminates and/or entertains. Poetry more often penetrates to the soul, therefore, while prose usually slops around in the brain. Archetypes, finally. Poems drip more especially with compact, mythological power than do prose stories and editorials. I may be wrong, but I doubt it.

Now if this is true, it is asked, why does anyone—reader or writer—confound herself with prose; and is *confound* the best word here? (Does it need to be the best word?) Well, as it was once untangled for me by an old charter boat captain out of Islamorada: "Prose is the groupers and poetry is the swordfish. You can catch and eat both. One jumps a hell of a lot and is very beautiful. But even the most snobby and bookish landlubber would get sick of a steady diet of swordfish."

Prose—adopted from the French *prose* and an adaptation of the Latin *prosa*—is defined in the *OED* as the ordinary form of written or spoken language, without metrical structure. This definition arguably contrasts with the work of some writers and critics, and of course the James Joyce of *Ulysses* and later is a terrifying exception to the "metrical structure" debate.

Recently, at a satellite event of the Modern Language Association, I heard it maintained that the differences today between most literary prose and poetry are minuscule and might be invisible if not for the poets' annoying and yet withstanding tradition of scattering their words on the page in forms that still resemble stanzas. To illustrate, two young professors from a famous Midwest M.F.A. program took a passage from a contemporary novel and rendered it in loose, irregular verse paragraphs. They Xeroxed their poem and distributed it to the audience of educators and scholars. Loathsome and behold, nearly all of those present but the inebriated believed the piece to be a real poem. Even some of the drunks thought it was just a Bob Dylan lyric. Now see this near plagiarized thing for yourself:

A ROLLING HITCH

Quoyle
got the water jug
from the car. In fifteen
minutes they were drinking
out of the soda cans,
scalding tea
that tasted of smoke and orangeade.

. . . Fog shuddered against their faces.
The aunt's trouser cuffs
snapped in the wind.

Ochre brilliance
suffused the tattered fog,
disclosed the bay,
smothered it.

[From *The Shipping News,* by E. Annie Proulx]

Amazing, right? Wrong. What this proves ultimately and again is that tenure-track profs will hunker down to very desperate tricks when forced to upgrade their curriculum vitae. And while this middle-aged Dr. Schrapnel was not fooled, and therefore unwowed, by such super English major gymnastics, the erudite audience (many of them bifocaled or shawled or wearing ties) seemed not to detect, or object to, the fundamental crapola aflight, accepting the premise that very modern prose and poetry are verily indistinguishable.

Holy trash can, readers and scholars! Is it really a wonder why teacher salaries are scarcely competitive with that of a mid-management position at the Outback Steakhouse? Or genuinely surprised, are you, that few outsiders (noneducation persons) care enough to do anything about it? Isn't it a shame that even one of your fellow professors can bring himself to scribble only a bunch of clichés when the issue comes up again?

But I can remember feeling something like cataclysmic dismay in 1991, the last time I taught a university freshman comp class, and only two of the twenty students had heard of Coleridge.

Isn't American education in straits perilous enough without an adjunct professor like you throwing rocks at the boat? One might expect to hear Republicans and Limbaughites engaging in such mindless rhetoric—fraught with illogic and half-truths—but . . . Finally, the distinctions between prose and poetry are more instinctual than formulaic, more metaphysical than logical. Seriously fine writers know this and do not spill cold ink over it, or try to burn down good houses. Where is your brain?

Aristotle Sardanapalus
Athens, Ga.

OK. But do *you* really think there's no difference between poems and the other stuff? I went to six poetry slams at restaurants and bars last month, where people mostly with GEDs and dysfunctional pasts get up and read their own poems. Most of it sounded like Allen Ginsberg without a vocabulary. A lot of the readers tried to be dramatic and shouted and cursed their way through some bad ideas. I know that I'm no poet, and now I know you couldn't pay me to be one.

Sandy Shingles
Kew Gardens, N.Y.

What's the difference what you think about poetry and prose? Furthermore, what *do* you think? The thesis of your essay eludes me; and not all English teachers are full of crap. Even you, at times, must get something right. But when?

H. D. Chaucersmith,
Panama City, Fla.

Much to my horror, I find myself agreeing with the overview of your "Groupers and Swordfish" column, if in fact I decipher it accurately. Indeed teacher salaries are not competitive with those of most of today's professions; and that is responsible for the high percentage of the excellent students who opt not for education careers. But dumping more money into salary coffers won't make better teachers of the modest dullards already entrenched. Free, state-funded lobotomies may help some systems; and many systems could help themselves by raising, rather than lowering, academic standards, thus shrinking enrollments and perhaps making it easier to weed out marginal instructional personnel. Radical perhaps, but as your Bob Dylan writes, "When you ain't got nothin' you got nothin' to lose."

Dr. Richard L. Skidmore, Chairman
Department of Economics
Everglades State University

Please write us when you become thoroughly serious and obsessed with a topic germane to American education and the liberal arts. We have been following your columns for years and almost relish your pop treatments of everything from Shakespeare to Mars to the proverbial kitchen sink. With a little added discipline, you may become important. Awaiting your query, which is certain to follow your rehabilitation.

Editors
W. W. Norton & Company
New York & London

 AMONG CRETINS

As keynote speaker at a recent regional convention of the International Society for Unbelievably Preposterous Prose (IS-FUPP) I was obliged to juggle some cumbersome and passionate questions following my address. One plea particularly struck me—coming from a recent college graduate who looked normal, though slightly emaciated—as timely and especially desperate.

"How," he inquired, "since the editorial level of the American publishing industry is so amuck with ill-educated cretins . . . [gasp & swallow] how may a beginning literary author of merit and promise deal with the hundreds of mindless, form rejection slips that regularly fill his/her mailbox?"

I frowned, grinned, then took a great gulp of the Planter's Punch that I kept on the first shelf under the podium. Because I insisted on no garnish, the faithful of editors and writers present no doubt thought it was a harmless species of Snapple. I showed them.

Today I am here to show you, forever masochistic readers and writers. I began my reply by commenting on the young man's choice of the word *cretin,* which immediately recalls D. H. Lawrence's repulsion for pornographic books: "They are either so ugly they make you ill, or so fatuous you can't imagine anybody but a cretin or a moron reading them, or writing them."

A cretin is a deformed idiot. It is from the nineteenth-century French, *crestin,* or Christian. The old usage was not intended to be an ethnic or denominational insult, however, as the point was to emphasize that despite their lessened physical and mental traits, certain deranged dwarfs (cretins) were nevertheless human and Christian.

The contemporary offspring of cretin are: *cretinous*—computerese for that which is wrong, inoperative, or wretchedly designed; *cretinoid*—student slang meaning spastic, or screwed to the

gills. More sadly, *cretinism,* a congenital condition caused by pre-
natal deficiency of thyroid hormones, is also called congenital
myxedema, which is characterized by dwarfism, mental retarda-
tion, dystrophy of the bones, and low basal metabolism.

At this point, mayhap, some readers are anticipating another
reference to TV intellectual Rush Limbaugh. But the Adventure
must press on.

To return to the specifics of the young writer's question, always remember that with the term *publishing industry* the dominant conceptual component is the word *industry.* That is, publishing is big business, one that eats and breathes that which will make
it lots of money. Period. And literature, as one perhaps comes to
understand it in college English classes and writers' workshops,
does not sell well nowadays, maybe never did in this century. Or
at least it rarely provides an author with a comfortable existence
during his/her lifetime. I may be wrong, but I doubt it.

So . . . if you're going to write a book that is easily publishable
(marketable), keep it simple, devoid of symbolism, archetypal
patterns, and too many multisyllabic words. Throw in a little sex
and swearing. Keep subplots and intrigue minimal and buffoon-
friendly. Do not call your villain Uriah Heep or Simon Legree.
Also, if you can pass yourself (author) out as a woman of minority
background, with an erratic past and unpredictable future (due to
a life-threatening ailment or a mental disorder *or both!*), you are
in the door, baby. But if you fancy yourself a poet, get used to hun-
ger, ridicule, and "huh?"

And really, as for the Big R (rejection), realize that there is no
excuse for going forever unpublished if you are persistent and obsessed. You can try, as it goes in the vernacular, sucking up to the
right people at writers' conferences. And there is always that network of hacks and wannabees found on various computer bulletin
boards. Or if you are almost independently wealthy, write to van-
ity/subsidy presses, who will be on you like gulls to tourist lunch-
ers at the mere sight of your postcard. And don't forget to subscribe to one of the hundreds of "literary magazines" out there
that publish only "work" by their subscribers. In short, if you can
pay for it, someone will publish it somewhere, no matter who, what,
when, why, or how.

But if it helps to think of editors and their slushpile underlings as cretins, do so. And how about a malignant synonym for literary agents too? To become a published author you need not possess real talent. If you know the right people, and/or fondle the correct buttocks, you will gain notice and royalty. Also, if you are unbelievably lucky and somehow drop your manuscript on the right desk at the right time . . . well, think of all of those postage stamps as lottery tickets, and try not to think of Shirley Jackson's most popular short story or you will scuttle the context, to say nothing of your self-esteem.

And in conclusion, don't take the suicide road, as a number of authors have done after years of frustration and rejection. For if you stop your heart or blow out your brains, you are no better than the cretins with whom you wish to cuddle. If you are good, someone will notice someday. Whether or not you will be around is another set of dynamics. I always plan on being around.

Your sour grapes remarks about publishers and editors are a disgrace, and a naive conception of what goes on at the editorial level of a major publishing house. It sounds like you've had your share of rejections, literary and otherwise. I can see why. Rather than giving young writers stupid advice, you should get a job at a car wash.

Rudolph Hearst IV
New York

It's not easy being an editor, at any level. You read so much crap that after a while you begin to wonder what the difference is between good and bad writing. Then you read something like "Adventures in Entomology" and you question the wisdom of mandatory education and the open-door policy at so many American colleges. As a poet once said, a little learning is a dangerous thing. In your case, it's just plain ridiculous.

Elaine Grebstein-Grubstein
New York

ISFUPP is grateful for your participation at our southeast regional convention and the reference in your stupendous column. The young writer you advised is now missing, although Knopf accepted his first novel just prior to his strange disappearance, his living companion tells us. We do not know if he knows. And I have some pills that will ease your misanthropy.

Françoise Dubonnet
ISFUPP, Atlanta

I think you're right. None of my good short stories has impressed any editors. So I wrote a deliberately terrible, perverted story that culminated in an interracial, interspecies orgy at a big-city zoo on Memorial Day. It's called "Eat Shit and Bark at the Moon." *Playboy* paid $3,000 for it, and the *Georgia Review*, in an effort to loosen up their image, says they'll pay the same for second serial rights. Now I guess I need an agent.

Misty McGraw
Ketchum, Idaho

In your next Planter's Punch, try floating some eggs from the shortnose American garfish, which I can send you. They look just like caviar. And they make a cute, minuscule garnish that will really get you going. Suck them down all at once, brother.

Boris on the Bayou

(Editorial Note: Gar eggs are deadly poisonous. This is the closest thing to a death threat that Dr. Schrapnel has received this year.)

"TED NUGENT MUST DIE!"

That flamboyant ecowarrior Forrest Jones phoned me last week after learning that the FBI had removed its tap from my lines. Defiled if I know how he knows of those things before I do, but that is one of Jones's knacks, you see. Some people just know and are therefore grandly destined. Destined, that is, to elude forever the tentacles of human correctional institutions. Jones, anyway, told me to watch my post office box for something.

There can be no smooth, transitional paragraph here.

Forrest Jones mailed me one thousand black-on-white bumper stickers that declare: "Ted Nugent Must Die!" Now, I do not know much about Ted Nugent, except that he is an aging rock star of modest achievement and is sometimes called the Motor City Madman with Attitude. Last summer, some medium of media announced that this long-haired, sunglassed musician—who publishes a hunting magazine—landed a radio talk show wherein he planned to glorify over the airwaves the murdering of small and large game mammals. Well, Forrest Jones, being an antihunting (sport hunting) paladin as well as the supreme monkeywrencher, is ticked. Hence his bumperobilia, "Ted Nugent Must Die!"

Of course, by now all of this information on the sadism of Ted Nugent is moldy news to most. And whatever Nugent wishes to shoot is his business, and that of millions of others, it will seem. But he needs to know that when he riles Forrest Jones and his dangerous followers, well . . . as Jones himself somewhat cryptically asks, "Heavens to murgatroyd, must I boondock this noisy creep too?"

While the question is terribly rhetorical, the diction is verily charming and hauntingly consistent, just like Forrest Jones. "Heavens to murgatroyd!" is the signature exclamation of the famous cartoon lion Snagglepuss. A murgatroyd is a defective wink, as in a contest of tiddlywinks, the table game that involves snapping plastic disks into a cup. A murgatroyd is flat on both sides. Pog is a contemporary derivative of tiddlywinks. In pog, the cardboard circles from the inside of certain milk bottle caps are used something like winks. What Snagglepuss means when he utters "Heavens to murgatroyd!" cannot be ascertained by logic, metaphysics, or Ouija board; but what Forrest Jones means when he uses *boondock* as a verb is threatening. In tiddlywinks, one boondocks an opponent's wink by shooting it off the playing surface. The sense is similar to the phrase "out in the boondocks" or a place of distance far from the madding masses, commercial or spiritual.

So does Forrest Jones plan to boondock Ted Nugent? Who knows? But Jones is suspected of maiming bear poachers in Vermont. Theory has it too, along with some fresh posters hanging in my local courthouse lobby, that Forrest Jones knows something about the reputed assassination of those three Mitsubishi executives last year in St. Louis, for reasons said to have something to do with their company's well-known rape of Asian rain forest. Whatever, color Mr. Jones a bright green.

If Forrest Jones boondocks Ted Nugent, what a riot it will stir in the international press, rivaling anything President Clinton has done and anything TV intellectual Rush Limbaugh says Mr. Clinton has done. The boondocking of Nugent might eclipse even the Simpson (as in O.J.) "trial." And given the Republican outgrowth in Washington, D.C., such a major boondocking could create serious backlash against environmentalists everywhere. I hope that does not happen. Let us not have even one Greenie stoop to terrorism. Let us hope that Forrest Jones is just sporting his pronounced sense of black humor this time. And will someone please come to my office and take these bumper stickers off my hands, so to speak. They would look unprofessorial on my Jeep.

Thanks for the tip. But I doubt if some dirt-ball green-freak can get close enough to Mr. Nugent to inflict any damage. Mr. Nugent is a wealthy, influential sportsman whose security procedures are state of the art. Your Mr. Jones and his accomplices are the ones who'd best tuck their tails between their legs and head for the hills.

Anonymous
FBI, Chicago

You should have indulged us with more elaboration on murgatroyds, which are considered defective because they are flat on both sides. A good wink has a slightly convex surface. The adult version of tiddlywinks was perfected by Cambridge undergraduates around 1955, although primitive forms of the game abounded in England from the mid to late 1800s. The 1885 *Montgomery Ward Catalog* advertises "Tiddledy Winks," and so on.

John Major
London, U.K.

The word *tiddly* is late nineteenth-century British slang for slightly drunk, while *tiddlywink* was a saloon or tavern operating illegally. There is more to this connection with clandestine drinking, beyond moderation, of alcoholic beverages. But I believe I have made my point.

Gladys
Paris, Pa.

Your propensity for alarmist baloney continues. But really, if that green weenie friend of yours kidnaps or kills a washed-up rock star who likes to hunt, so what? At the rate humanity is going, we'll never be able to get out of this solar system before our sun goes supernova anyway. That's why I'll play an occasional game of tiddlywinks with my kids; but I'll be damned if I'm going to start to read *Remembrance of Things Past*. I am not an existentialist, but you'd be surprised.

Kenneth Pabst
Drudgery Hill, N.H.

Chapter 3 of *The Grapes of Wrath,* the scene where the redneck truck driver tries to run over the turtle crossing the road, contains the following: "His front wheel struck the edge of the shell, flipped the turtle like a tiddly-wink." The turtle survives. This is one of the greatest symbolic passages in all of American literature. The simile is especially rich if you have ever won at tiddlywinks. Steinbeck might have written "boondocked" instead of "flipped" but chose to temper the image, unlike your Forrest Jones, who, as environmentalists go, is truly a murgatroyd when it comes to diction.

Chester H. Berlin
San Jose, Calif.

♣ MONSTER MASH REVISITED

Modred Allen Hopswitch, my former university colleague, retired recently from a college in Minnesota. Now he lives at an insane asylum, strapped in traditional attire in a soft room. I visited the once articulate and energetic etymologist last month to find out what snapped. To be brief, he says he sees monsters. He babbles a few nearly coherent sentences, then shrieks, "Monsters! Monsters! Monsters!"

Monster, etymologically, springs from the Latin *monstrum,* a derivative of the verb *monere,* to warn. Originally the sense is "warning of misfortune, evil omen." According to John Ayto, "*monstrum* was transferred to the sort of thing that could function as such an omen—a 'prodigy,' or a 'misshapen or horrifying creature'—whence the meaning of English *monster.*"

"What kinds of monsters, Moe?" I had to know. He wriggled and winced (as if in the throes of a horrible hallucination), writhed about, terror in his eyes, like a hooked eel on the banks of the Thames. Then he focused on the fluorescent ceiling fixture and announced in an ominous tone: "Windigo! Yehwe Zogbanu! Dungavenhooter! Goonswoggle!"

Then he passed out.

Oh, what a noble mind is here o'erthrown, I said to myself.

Now, damned if I know how or why M. A. Hopswitch hitched a ride on the Twilight Zone Trolley, but I do know something of the nomenclatures he spouted on that unnerving afternoon before he lost consciousness, among other things. All of those names denote monsters from various folk and mythic literatures. Among early Minnesota settlers, Windigo was a fifteen-foot-tall spirit who dressed in robes of dazzling white. Windigo had a star in the middle of its forehead, and its sighting was always a prelude to a death in the family. In addition, Windigo (also Wendigo or Wiendigo) is the cannibalistic spirit of Algonquian lore that roams the forest and devours people. A lost hunter who resorts to eating human flesh is believed to become a Windigo or an investigative reporter. Similarly, Yehwe Zogbanu, a giant of Dahomean myth, is a forest-dwelling creature that sports thirty horns and is forever threatening hunters. Professor Hopswitch, a student of North American legend and all that, was no doubt aware of the tales of these monsters. And as an avid deer hunter, could it be that he thought he experienced a close encounter with one on the weekend outing that preceded by only seven days his trip to the boofo box?

So if all of this is not enough to keep you out of the woods, be cautioned too that the ecowarrior Forrest Jones was last seen in Minnesota harassing—that is, shooting the hands off—wolf poachers. This is not a pretty column today, but it gets worse.

Dungavenhooter is a reptile resembling an alligator with a nose the size of truck tires and nasal cavities to match. Once ranging from Maine to Montana, Dungavenhooter was the scourge of logging camps and communities. In Henry H. Tryon's scantily circulated *Fearsome Critters* (circa 1933) there is the following terrifying account of typical Dungavenhooter behavior.

"Concealing itself with Satanic cunning behind a whiffle bush, the Dungavenhooter awaits the passing logger. On coming within reach of the dreadful tail, the victim is knocked senseless and then pounded steadily until he becomes entirely gaseous, whereat he is greedily inhaled through the wide nostrils. . . . Rum sodden prey is sought with especial eagerness" (quoted from *Dickson's Word Treasury,* Wiley & Sons, 1992).

But as any good Diffusionist should know, the legend can be tracked to merry Middle English England. For in Chaucer's ribald and dubious Canterbury piece "The Reprobate's Tale," there are the quizzical lines that follow the pastoral knee-kissing scene so much admired by D. H. Lawrence.

And now, sweete love, I mus for to shoote
With mine arrow the damned Dungaven-hootere,

Air it may smooshe like a froge
Me frende who fells the greate logge.

It is a rare instance of what has come to be known to folklorists as the Hoover-beast trickster archetype. And there are additional motifs here yet to be numbered and entered in Stith Thompson's motif index. Scholarship, after all, is no hare. Reminiscent of Dungavenhooter is the Goonswoggle of coastal southwest Florida. Environmental activists describe the Goonswoggle as possessing the head of the endangered American crocodile and the body of Henry David Thoreau. Goonswoggles walk upright and prey on tourists and retired transplants to the sunshine state. The presence of a Goonswoggle in an undeveloped waterfront area sends county governments into a swoon and a re-zoning shuffle, first opening up the supposedly plagued lands to unrestricted hunting, then changing (within a year) the zoning to suit the long, slimy arms of real estate developers. How it is that Modred Allen Hopswitch knows of this legendary devourer of snowbirds . . . oh hell, let speculation fly!

And what, last, does it all mean? What rough beast slouches presently in the tortured cavities of Moe's mind? When again will it pounce? Or if it's a virus, is it contagious? And is it true that somewhere in a remote niche of Washington state, Forrest Jones's followers have initiated a captive breeding program for the Dungavenhooter?

And as I queried many moons ago, could it be that our great American melting pot develops a stress fracture? I may be wrong, but I doubt it.

Alarmist rhetoric like your monster column should be censored. And although I feel for your deranged friend Professor Hopswitch, I have to hope that his caretakers at the funny farm make room for you also. Your column has gone so spiritually awry of late that it cannot be long before you get a call from one of those radical antiabortion assassins, or perhaps receive a gift certificate for a free visit with Dr. Kevorkian, or something like this.

Silas M. Mather
Salem, Mass.

Yes, Schrapnel, there are creatures out there even more horrifying and deliciously imposing than you hint at in your Adventures. Take a walk sometime on the wooded hills. If you stroll naked you can see more. I think I love you.

Natasha Lucretia Brains
Stephens City, Va.

The comparative mythologist Joseph Campbell is said to claim to have seen Windigo just three days before his death. And his supposed last words (Campbell's)—"Moose, Indian"—echo the deathbed syllables of H. D. Thoreau. What do you think it signifies, you sexist slime mutton? If this letter makes no sense to you, consider yourself my hero.

Wendy Lightwood
Lightwood, N.M.

By using Ophelia's remark of Hamlet in the nunnery scene, "Oh, what a noble mind is here o'erthrown," you suggest that

Professor Hopswitch was your lover. I say you are a cranky gay blade who has blown his cover. Let's see who reads you now.

Mack Trucks
Vancouver, B.C.

Arch jerk of jerks! I spit on your column! I was with Moe Hopswitch on that "fateful" hunting trip to which you refer, and nothing happened. We saw no monsters. What are you, on hallucinogens again, you fraudulent, bogus, cry-wolf crackpot, syllable slobbering, apocalypse pushing, pseudointellectual, pompous-prosed, symbol-sucking freak? Once again you prove that a little (very little) research is a dangerous thing. And I want your readers to know that you chickened out on that flapdragon challenge, you cowardly, cretinous creep of a minion-muddled monstrosity!

Elvis Peebles
SUNY-Duluth

(Editorial Note: Elvis Peebles's latest book, The Curmudgeon's Guide to Gerard Manley Hopkins, *can be found on the bargain tables of most bookstores.)*

 POEM AS HEIMLICH MANEUVER

"I'm gonna read jew now some a my new pomes that are pretty radical and different. These pomes I write in what I call diabobic voice, which I don't have time to tell you what that is, but you can get a feel fer what I mean if I just read."

Thus Garth ———, popular California coffeehouse poet, prefaces the closing segment of his latest poetry slam appearance at Bistro de Juan Valdez, a growing mecca for contemporary verse buffs and recreational druggies near the campus of Georgetown University. BJV is one of the few stops on the poetry circuit that pays performers/readers in American currency (twenty-five to a hundred dollars a set) and not with beer, espresso, complimentary appetizer, a wine cooler, or a shot of Cuervo. On the night of Garth ———'s appearance, the room was sardine city, crawling with untenured profs and M.F.A. candidates, with a sprinkling of journalists and urban gang members.

But *diabobic* voice? I wondered. Then I remembered—*Burgess Unabridged,* by American humorist Gelett Burgess (1866–1951), who subtitled his 1914 work *A New Dictionary of Words You Have Always Needed.* Burgess defined *diabob* as "an object of amateur art; anything improbably decorated; hand-painted." *Diabobical* means "ugly, while pretending to be beautiful." Pampas grass dyed bright purple; ornamented, hand-painted trash cans, bean pots, and molasses jugs; the decorative fan adorned with Mount Fujiyama; pine cones spray-painted gold—these things are diabobical.

Therefore, I thought, to call one's verse voice *diabobic* rings pejorative, does it not? Or does the poet intend to be taken as a promoter of light verse, comic to satiric? Indeed when Garth ———

finished his reading with the short piece entitled "Honors Seminar, Fall Semester 1993," ambivalence tortured me.

> Astrid's currant lips
> or Gwen Devereaux's night eyes Yie! Yie! Yie!
> How absolute the slave is.
> I am dead if I look at her again. Oh, it will
> kill me dead, so dead I'll
> stink before I hit the ground,
> so Mother soft,
> dearth Earth . . . Mommy!

A lightning bolt of laughter arose from my chest and I spewed a small half swallow of Irish coffee across the linen tablecloth, happily dark green. Many in the audience around me chuckled and applauded heartily, so confirming my hunch that the poet was dialing for laughs. Hmmm, I reflected privately. There is, to be sure, some ugly pretending in the cadences of Garth ——, but beauteous truth and irony, sage and symptom, worm forth too. The poet, in theory and artifice, perhaps twists Burgess's pejorative toward the affirmative, like the corkscrew voice of the satirist.

A short conversation with Garth —— and his biographer and traveling companion, the poetess/critic Lolita Marcia Drizell, illuminates. Voilà!

"Diabobic voice," explains Garth ——, "is a side effect of a serious poetry done with cunning and grinning. It is not light verse, however, in the sense of Ogden Nash, Richard Armour, or *MAD* magazine, because its design is to engage perception and smile by the daring nature of its language, mixed with the latent horrors of various images and near images. Wallace Stevens often verged on diabobic voice, but he never succumbed unequivocally to that muse. I suppose it was his job that held him back. Afterall, how truly tragicomic is insurance work in the big picture? And tragicomedy is the principal chord in diabobic voice."

Immediately I wanted to ask Garth —— why his diction and syntax changes so dramatically when he leaves the podium and sits down to discuss poesie with a couple of critics, but Lolita

Marcia Drizell bludgeoned us with a memorable verbal thud and a thick cloud of Virginia Slims.

"Isn't truth a goddamn beauty? What he means is, there are so many writers and poets in print now, gobs of books, and most of them are of dismal vision. It's necessary to keep in mind, however, that in any age, only about 10 percent of what's published endures, or will still be around in, say, forty years. So the published things nowadays, most, are so much poorly chewed beef liver, rich in gristle, if you can follow my metaphor. Gristle that becomes lodged in the throat of the reading public, which chokes willingly on it because the people believe they are trying to ingest literature, which is supposed to be good for them."

"Oh, so that's what you mean?" I asked Garth ———.

He beamed at Lolita and to me replied, "Indeed! Airways must be cleared. The gag bait that is a staple of the wheezing reading public, and of formal education, must be expelled. And diabobic voice, the muse behind my latest poems, is the spiritual Heimlich maneuver that contemporary verse—so hunched and heaving as it is—so pitifully needs. And do not call me iconoclastic, please."

More in the mood now for the proverbial small talk than for some two-fisted tirade—à la mode though it yet is—on the quality of American literature, I excused myself for a visit to the lavatory, but not before Garth could dig from his knapsack a full-color brochure for his newly founded Compost Writers Workshop, scheduled to run June through July somewhere along the banks of Lake Tahoe.

During the drive back to my hotel, I kept asking myself aloud, "What in the hell did they mean?"

"When quandaried," I once told a B+ literature student, "try something like Formalism, a close textual analysis of the poem. To hell with biography, the social milieu or the possibility that the author really is a posturing crackpot who took three years to earn the A.A. degree and once sold Amway."

But a semiformalist reading of "Honors Seminar" yields mixed meaning, you see. Lines 1 and 2 focus on the attracting features of two women, perhaps classmates of the author/speaker, who possess dark lips and dark eyes, respectively. But the "Yie! Yie! Yie!" jettisons the potentially erotic tenor of the opening into the realm of cowboy song. Next is an allusion to Hamlet's remark about the gravedigger—"How absolute the knave is"—as the Prince marvels at the quite literal answers of his comic counterpart. Here, though, the speaker is a "slave," perhaps confessing to the stifling effect of his classroom voyeurism or infatuation. Thus three lines into the Garth —— poem we are wondering about subject and theme.

Hyperbole enters. One more look at Astrid or Gwen, the speaker claims, will surely and swiftly kill him. There will ensue a surreal rate of decomposition, and the speaker will be a smelly, ugly corpse prior to contact with the earth, floor, or wherever. This detail seems to make appropriate the allusion to the gravedigger scene, but so what? For the final two lines pester us with befuddling Freudian and environmental images. The words "so Mother soft" do more than hint of Oedipal preoccupation, and the phrase "dearth Earth" literally connotes a planet on which all forms of sustenance are scarce, which leads to the final outcry, or lament, "Mommy!"

Does the poet sense here, then, that he should keep his mind on the seminar lecture and his eyes off his attractive classmates? Is failure in the breeze? Is the poet's dilemma false, or is it a metaphor that signals the death of our planet if humankind cannot focus collective attention upon more serious, primal, and ecological purposes? My guess is that the poem is another of those slithering, simpering cries for help, trying to break through to an archetypal plane. It is sophomoric confessional poetry that intuits a higher meaning in the situation but has to laugh. The poem (or poet) knows not where to go, so it (he) offers an Oedipal/ecological guffaw as a final yelp.

I may be wrong, but I doubt it. The poems of Garth —— are half poems actually, in need of some method to their madness, some revision and reworking. And although the poet invited me to lecture at his writers' workshop this summer, offering me a huge stipend, I've already promised some politicians and professors in and around Tallahassee that I would score CLAST essay exams then. It is my way of submersing myself in the destructive element in order to effect a rebirth.

In that delightful *Burgess Unabridged* he also coins *Gefoojet*— "an unnecessary thing . . . , something one ought to throw away, but doesn't . . . the god of unnecessary things." Here we have a sublime description of your column, as well as the identification of your muse.

Clark C. Clarke
East Lansing, Mich.

Your recurring declaration "I may be wrong, but I doubt it" is a poorly obfuscated plagiarism of "Often wrong but never in doubt," the professed motto of the great critic at SUNY, Buffalo, Leslie Fiedler. I heard Dr. Fiedler confess this credo in an address he delivered at Chautauqua in the late seventies. I believe the speech was entitled "After the Death of the Novel." That's all, folks!

Jan Lee Pan
Osaka, Japan

Who is Garth ———? Why are you belittling poetry readings now? Does contemporary literature really cause you to choke? How long have you been able to remain at one teaching job? What sort of editors take you seriously? When? Aren't you a nihilist?

Benjamin Franklin Hawkes
Philadelphia, Pa.

Having heard Garth —— read at the University of Southeastern West Virginia at Cabin Creek (USWVCC, in the hometown of retired NBA great Jerry West), I must respectfully disagree with your scathing overview of his work. He is a man of many deep metaphors that elude the typical not-so-careful listener with the near-cliché nature of their language and signature, along with those eternally urban rhythms that I like to liken, as an almost blasphemous, though terribly spiritualistic, marriage of meters, to the heartbeat of great forms ranging from Neo-Classical tropes to the bass parts in some early Motown recordings. While the artifice of Garth —— is seemingly supine yet monstrously eclectic, to say the least, it is the most proper focus of critics more formally trained in metaphormalistic modes of Deconstruction analysis as devised by Duke and Cambridge University scholars like Helen Penn-Richardson, Barnaby W. C. Etheridge, and Mack Frost. Having studied under all three professors, I could enlighten you and your ill-informed audience with regard to such critical dictum; but my pride and position will not allow me to stoop to a guest columnist spot in a lowbrow atrocity entitled "Adventures in Etymology." Therefore, you and your ilk must continue to wallow and babble in the sophomoric mire that you water. And please do not enroll in any of my classes.

Peter Tom Oldham
Lafayette University

Yes, so many poetry "slams" are dominated by hacks, losers, and slobs. Yes, the "literature" they promote is generally inferior and trite. But no! You and other "critics" have no right to belittle such performances. Beneath all of that posturing and bad writing are some sincere efforts to come to grips with literature and the serious nature of poetry and real life. It's better than sitting around doing drugs and alcohol, and it's usually better than reading things like your "Adventures in Entomology."

Carla Rhodes-Bell, MA
University of Chicago

The ranty tenor of your columns aside, Schrapnel, you do make some terribly perceptive observations week after week and so on. I suspect you are a passionate man of letters who tries at times to disguise his outrage and frustration with literary peers and colleagues with satire and the less accessible forms of irony and odd wit. Your recent exposure of the fraudulent coffeehouse scene, with its renegade profs and poetasters, is sure to garner bales of outcry and hate male; but there has always been merit and verity in the notion that everlasting literature is rarely common or mainstream. And you have as much right to detest bad writing and thinking as your readers have to deplore your sharp points of view. Democracy, then, is not so palatable for so many, and does it not seem that so many Americans secretly crave a switch to anarchy? Those "etymologies" of yours are often springboards into darker and ignored truths. You do not fool me.

Regina B. Stoker
Ironton, Ohio

# THE GIG IS UP

When browsing bookstore bins, I sometimes play a mind game that I call gigging. I will peruse a title and let ramification, denotation, and connotation float on the tide of my conscious/unconscious to and fro and toodley-doo. It can be whimsical and time-consuming. So if you arrive late at the mall and discover an especially intoxicating title, you could be ejected at nine. But if it be a nonmall book stop, the staff is usually more understanding, tolerant, eccentric, and as weary of Robert James Waller as you are. So, go ahead and gig.

Gigging with Frankie arrested me at Cole's last month. Now, the trick is, you do not touch the book or read anything on the jacket but the title. You are gigging. So you just imagine. Voilà. First, it seemed, *Gigging with Frankie* is another groupie's or musician's account of life on the road. *Gig* in its most current sense, and in musician jargon, means a job or engagement. But while *giggy* is seventeenth-century British slang for vulva or anus, the book is probably not the biography of another libertine.

Frankie, however, may be fond of frog legs. So the book could be one of those how-to-do-it things, no doubt appalling to the animal rights weenies. You know, *gig* is a three- to five-tine spear used to impale fish, frogs, snakes, and anything else incredible or edible. When gigging, according to the *Dictionary of American Regional English,* "The giggers go barefoot or don wading boots . . . and select a long and relatively narrow stretch of river leading to a pool of convenient shallowness."

Sounds like a Michener novel, I fear.

Well, one usually gigs at night. The nightlife is hardly idyllic. Imagine Frankie and the author on one dark eve confronting

Otissmocroke, the leviathan amphibian of Ozark and Cree legend whose adhesive tongue is said to be so huge as to be able to snatch a bull bison with one slap. Suppose that the book then becomes a gloomy chronicle ending with the death of Frankie, killed in battle, by Otissmocroke, when his gig breaks on the ominous chin of the monster. Yes, breaks! Oh, shades of the sword of Beowulf (Naegling) on his last dragon-slaying gig.

Then comes the funeral of Frankie—Lord of the Froggers, Earl of the Giggers—where he is carried by gig (a light two-wheeled one-horse carriage) and gigged (to move up and down along the river's edge) along the banks of his home river. The procession, because Frankie was no gig (a queer-looking figure . . . fool), is sometimes punctuated by high gig (fun, merriment, glee) and curiously attended by a score of Frankie's old gigs (flighty, giddy girls), who rankle the patience of the next-of-kin and Frankie's cranky widow.

The funereal finale is a grand one. Frankie's body and professional belongings are placed in a gig (a wooden box or chamber, with two compartments, one above the other) and are taken to the local lake, where it is loaded into a gig (a light, narrow, clinker-built ship's boat, adapted either for rowing or sailing) attended by two giggers, assorted symbolic animal parts, and a helmsman, who is Frankie's younger brother, Cletis. Cletis, of course, recites at the gathering at the lake, those lines from "The Yarn of the *Nancy Bell*"—

Oh, I am a cook and a captain bold,
And the mate of the Nancy brig,
And a bo'sun tight, and a midshipmite,
And the crew of the captain's gig.

But the somber and mythic tone of the funeral service is momentarily splashed when Frankie's longtime arch rival of the froggery, Regis Ronk, leaps from out of the lake and retorts—

There was an old person of Ealing,
Who was wholly devoid of good feeling;

He drove a small gig,
With three owls and a pig,
Which distressed all the people of Ealing.

Regis Ronk's attempt to gig (to befool, hoax) the proceedings offends many of the mourners, who wrestle him from the water, drag him screaming to a giant sycamore, and bind and gag him. They place a gig (a whipping top) on his large forehead and set it spinning. Then they tie a gig (a set of feathers arranged so as to revolve rapidly in the wind, for the purpose of attracting birds to a net) to an overhead branch. That will show him.

Appropriately, Frankie gigs (to ride or travel in a gig) on his last gig. As the ancient gig gigs away, the oarsmen stroke slowly and the oarlocks make a gig (a squeaking noise). It reminds me of what is perhaps the earliest recorded use of *gig* in English: "And all this hous was made of twigges. . . . this hous was also ful of gyges" (*The House of Fame*, Chaucer, 1384).

It's been a sad gig.

About to gig off to the local tavern and drink a toast to Gig Young, I am nevertheless jarred when the bookstore manager announces, "Hurry up please; it's time!"

They are closing. My gigging must halt.

You see, this is what happens to this language professional about town, when I OD on the *OED*. I overextend the bookstore. I get one gig (demerit) for not buying a book.

I need a vacation.

Don't you have a good gig now? And here is some good reply for a change. We are in the midst of compiling a new, in-house anthology for Freshman Composition I at Paltry Community College. Your essay on *gig* we would like to include in the "process analysis" chapter. Our Business Department just struck oil with the campus well, which is managed by students, so just name your price.

Clement W. Vaig
Floydada, Tex.

Hey dude! That's my book you gigged in your column. Your version is stupid. *Gigging with Frankie* is my side of the seamy rock and metal concert circuit with Frankie Fellatio, lead guitarist for the now defunct group Goose Grandma. I was the drummer. You'll be hearing from my lawyer.

Dowling Botz
Hannibal, Mo.

Gigging with Frankie is not as screwy as you imagine, and my attorney encourages me to sue you for slander. The book contains some of my late husband's favorite recipes for frog legs and frog leg gumbo. I am referring to Frankie Avalon, the once renowned chef at the Hotel Ribit in New Orleans. See you in court.

Annette Avalon
Vinton, La.

Twice in the past months you have cast aspersions upon the finest novella of the modern age, *The Bridges of Madison County*, by Robert James Waller. Having read the book six times, and having listened to Mr. Waller's wonderful recording of the songs of Madison County, I am forced to agree that you are indeed the tasteless cur that so many of your readers contend you are in their many letters. Mr. Waller is no doubt the next Jimmy Buffett of the art world, a truly double-threat genius who excels at both fiction and musical composition. It is you who have a problem, not today's literary audience. You might try going back to college to figure out what it is you missed there that could have caused you to become so devoid of critical insight.

Lawrence T. Freud
Fancy Gap, Va.

THE HEDGES OF LIVINGSTON COUNTY

"For most of its long history in English, *literate* has meant 'familiar with literature,' " reminds a usage note in *The American Heritage Dictionary*, "or more generally, 'well-educated, learned'; it is only during the last hundred years that it has also come to refer to the basic ability to read and write."

Even lexicography illiterates might guess from the above observation that some words and their conceptual worlds get watered down over the ages. Take literature (please). What does it mean to be "familiar with literature"? What is literature, anyway? Or as a 1982 Leslie Fiedler title asks, *What Was Literature?* To most readers of these Adventures, literature is the word "applied to writing which has claim to consideration on the ground of beauty of form or emotional effect." So says *The Oxford English Dictionary*. And the *AHD* defines literature as, "1. A body of writing in prose or verse. 2. Imaginative or creative writing especially of recognized artistic value. . . . 5. Printed material." Note the dilation of the definition and a consequent effect of something like a language version of the law of diminishing returns; or perhaps we have a linguistic lumbering toward the lowest common denominator. My flashy former colleague Martha Louise Carrier, who failed Linguistics 325 to specialize in the Beat Poets, explains this phenomenon thus: "Wow, man! I mean, words really do suck. By that metaphor I mean they—words—tend to hooverize their domain through so much use. That is, good words develop a vacuum of their own, whereby during generations of use and misuse they suck in more and more bourgeois debris that bulges their original or intended denotations at the expense of precision. *Literature* is an example of this strange unnamed law. *Literature,* to nearly all literate people, used to mean writing of special artistic merit. Now you hear about the 'literature' on the labels of soup cans, which dispatches nutritional misinformation."

And while Martha Louise has her *say* with words, etymology gives no rhyme or reason why *literature* has come to encompass the things that it does. *Literature* is from the Latin *littera*, or letter, and *literatus*, meaning to have knowledge of letters. A person of letters is a writer of literature, in theory, and there you have it in the proverbial pea pod. But why, when you call the distribution center to ask why your new cellular phone does not do what you thought it would do, does the person in the warranty department ask, "Have you read all of your literature?"

"Yes. In fact, I just finished *The Grapes of Wrath*, for the second time, an hour ago."

For twenty-five cents a minute (ninety-nine cents for long distance), you would think the helping voice could employ words with fewer syllables, like *book*, or *manual* (if not a zealous feminist). But that's just the way capitalism goes.

So to the more pressing phenom of expanding definition. Recall my 1993 essay "Romanticism Now and Then" and the section entitled "The Death of Everything." There I quote pop language maven William Safire thus: "After enough time, words come to mean what most people think they mean, not what we say they ought to mean." For so many people, there are no snugglies in those words. And if you think you will find a definition of literature in a specialized reference book like Holman's *A Handbook to Literature*, you are wrong. In those 500-plus pages of definitions, there is no definition of literature, L or elsewhere. Now, if you believe this piece is going nowhere on impulse power, well, just read on.

Novels, most agree, are literature. And in the last quarter century of American literary history, two novels that have sold millions and millions of copies are Richard Bach's *Jonathan Livingston Seagull* and *The Bridges of Madison County*, by Robert James Waller. Brace yourself, particularly if you have not read either book. For as you must know, these two little volumes have received almost unanimous, merciless, and unmitigated trashing and thrashing from reviewers, critics, and English teachers. Yes, in spite of their unparalleled achievements as best-sellers, *JLS* and

Bridges still inspire terrific loathing in the gamut of literature experts that the American majority has come to know and ignore. Leslie Fiedler, scholar and university professor, calls *JLS* "an absolutely tawdry and miserable novel which does not work on any level." Of Waller's works, New York reviewer Michiko Kakutani asks, "What is the appeal of these books? Waller's novels read as if they had been churned out by a word processor with scenes culled from soap operas, B movies and easy-listening songs written in language lifted from Hemingway parody contests and Playboy [*sic*] picture captions."

What's an inquiring reader to do?

"Well, uh," I can hear a higher education English prof begin to explain, "those books are what we call popular literature, a marijuana for the masses, if you will. But certainly we must realize that there is a profound difference, in mere terms of scope, between *Jonathan Livingston Seagull* and, well, *Moby-Dick,* both of which, on one plane, are sea novels. I am not yet convinced, however, that there is great dissimilarity between Mr. Waller's first book and, perhaps, *Tess of the D'Urbervilles,* both of which are tragic romances and abominably tedious movies."

Hrrumph and forsooth.

So. Literature today means so many things besides Virgil, Shakespeare, Jane Austen, Robert Frost, Toni Morrison, E. Annie Proulx, Saul Bellow, and so on. Popular literature is not literature literature, you see. *JLS* and *Bridges* are not art novels—those books read for, and explained in, English classes . . . well, most English classes. If you are literate, that means you can read, period. If things ain't what they used to be, words are things too. The mainstream has overflowed its banks and there is no chance that those waters of bourgeois dilution will fall back. It happens, as you may already be cognizant.

Yet it remains for us to name this unnamed law of lexicographic evolution by which some words become much more than what they were. Let us call it the Law of Denotative Explosion and realize that nearly anything that is conveyed through the myriad potential of alphabets is now literature. Yes, the walls have come tumbling down, and they cannot be mended. Those good fences which may once have made good neighbors, or at least kept the

Philistines from storming the library (or overturning the book-mobile)—oh, the fences are in terminal disrepair. Everybody is everywhere into everything. It is no longer multiculturalism; it is anticulturalism! What's a fan of belle lettres, a student of the canonical tradition, to do?

Oh, saddened Adventurers . . . the answer is in the following parable, related to me by Geoffrey W. Crayon (former editor of *Modern Philology*), who heard it at a seminar in Montreal. Behold: The ghost of Christos Kahounos, Ph.D., it is said, haunts the dank and musty PR to PS stacks on the seventh floor of the Grace Gorgon Memorial Library at Odin and Hermes University. Every year since his violent death by water in 1979. (Dr. Kahounos climbed a ladder and placed his mouth over a ceiling sprinkler fixture to show his class in the modern novel "What a big-mouth is Gore Vidal!" To the professor's extreme bad luck, smoke from a nearby bonfire blew in an open window and set off the sprinkler system, from which the raging doctor was unable to detach himself.) Dr. Kahounos's ghost has appeared to a graduate student in English on a day during the month of April, around 10:00 P.M., in the stacks of the old library. On April 15, 1984, the hapless student was Mary Magdalene Gandhi, who was researching her thesis "The Definition of Culture in Muriel Rukeyser's Clerihews." Suddenly and darkly aware of the specter professor's presence and of his reputation as a late advocate of the New Humanism, the quivering student asked, "What do you think of Western Culture?"

The spirit grinned, then declared with Dolby-quality resonance, "It sounds like a good idea."

There was a soft thud. Ms. Gandhi was discovered at midnight, by a security guard, lying half conscious in a puddle of bootlegged Diet Dr. Pepper, muttering the quizzical question and answer in various tongues.

"Was hast du von dem westlichen Kultur gedacht?"

"Es scheint eine gute Idee zu sein."

"Que pensez-vous de la culture occidental?"

"Ça me semble être une bonne idée."

"Yo mon, doo streit cool oxydent?"

"Yo coolala, coola coola moizy!"   And so on.

You tease us, Schrapnel. The conclusion to "The Hedges of Livingston County," with its plagiarized parable, smacks of the nonsensical, cop-out approach to poetry taken by John Keats at the end of "Ode on a Grecian Urn." Does anyone truly know what the hell "Beauty is truth, truth beauty" actually means in or out of the context of the poem? I hesitate to solicit your answer seriously. As for your Law of Denotative Explosion, you cannot call it a law, because a substantial majority of English words have not expanded in meaning so much as to become almost meaningless. Your columns, however, do lean that way.

Bernard G. Goldfarb
Queens, N.Y.

According to pop lexicographer Paul Dickson, a *counterword* is a word that has lost its original meaning through overuse and, I suppose, misuse. For example, *great* originally meant thick or coarse. *Cool* is another counterword. You might more accurately phrase your observation of expanding meaning, then, Counterword Cholera, for it is an infectious lexicographic phenomenon that is rarely less than lamentable to the truly literate.

Otto Von Himmelslip III
San Francisco, Calif.

Leave it to you to try to understand literature by way of novels that are (as they say in the vernacular) total bullshit. Bach and Waller write garbage. Those who read them and like it are tasteless dolts. Writers like you who still give such pulp feces some serious ink do nothing to assist the arts, literary or otherwise, in this their time of need. The Republicans are coming! The Republicans are coming! You could be next.

Fay Jameson-Green
Iowa City

What happened, Schrapnel? Did you bite off more than your little literary mouth could chew? That was an awfully stupid way to end your column. Obviously you don't know how to define literature, not that anyone cares whether you do. Your conclusion reminds me of the moronic way Philip Freneau ends "The Wild Honeysuckle," one of the worst poems in colonial American literature: "The space between is but an hour, / The frail duration of a flower." I suppose that this vague and trite observation of the transient beauty of nature is charming to some, if that is what Freneau is getting at. Keats uses a similar dodge at the end of "Ode on a Grecian Urn," another instance of magnanimous obfuscation. What you prove, then, is that some of the tricks that poets use when they back themselves into a metaphysical corner can be likewise employed by dim-witted prose writers. In other words, when you really don't know what in the world you are saying, or why, just toss them a glittering, hot red herring and call it a parable.

Tert C. Walton
Williamsburg, Va.

Your complaint about the mutability of language is like the Eskimo who bemoans having to walk over ice and snow. What is the point? Or as a vernacular observation goes: it comes with the territory. Some happenings are so inevitable or predestined that to ask why is irrational. The word *art* has not had it any easier than *literature*. When one reads headlines like "Mad Magazine Art Expected to Go for Millions at Auction,"

The Hedges of Livingston County   133

she realizes that what *art* means to many people has nothing to do with Rembrandt, Rubens, Whistler, Picasso, Cassatt, even Dali. So just quit whining and try to use more of your brain. Certainly a person who calls the words on the sides of cereal boxes "literature," or whatever covers the front of the box "art," could care less about "The Whiteness of the Whale" or *Watson and the Shark.* Don't encourage such degenerates to try to do more. Genuine art, or literature, has never been a supermarket commodity; and for that, those of us who love and appreciate such creations should be grateful and quiet. Oh, now I see I have ranted and rambled along just as you do, and it gives me shame.

Elise M. Degenneres
Versailles & New York

Exquisite snobbery such as yours would be deserving of some kind of award if it were not laced with idiocy. How one is to understand the word *literature,* when one reads or hears it, is determined by context. What one gets from reading literature (art novels) is determined by experience and education. It exasperates me to hear you fuss so.

C. Everett Mailer, Ph.D.
Howard University

Conservative sniffling like "The Hedges of Livingston County" worries me. Republicans and Bible boomers are always looking out for anything that could be interpreted as criticism of the current state of the arts. Even a bizarre analyst like you can furnish, albeit unwittingly, the antiarts movement in Washington with statistics and opinions that could sway additional cuts in NEH funds and arts programs in general. It would be noble and helpful of you to retire and stop writing. Literature needs a sane friend or two now, and I am not sure what you are.

Agnes St. Agnes-Dawson
Doom Gulch, N.M.

My research with some nineteenth-century English manuscripts lately attributed to Charles Dickens has uncovered an unpublished novella entitled *The Man Who Would Fart at Art.* It is an unfinished tale wherein a grinning, gray-haired villain named Newton Fig Gingrich (NFG for short) rallies many of Britain's most wealthy and influential clergy, businessmen, and politicians to join a censorship movement that aims to rid the country of books, paintings, and sculptures that are not based on the Bible. Leave it to Dickens to create another unforgettably loathsome antagonist of pure bile and mindless cunning. I suspect the story ends with the overthrow of Gingrich and his motley friends, but one never really knows with late Dickens, just as one cannot be sure why life sometimes imitates art, if it does.

James F. Allen
Puddin-on-Jello, G.B.

TOM ATE/SLEPT HERE

Planchet Defoliation is a new mode of literary criticism being taught and practiced at schools throughout the southeastern United States. To make the method work for you, you need a 486 Windows application computer (at least), a graduate degree in English, and a Ouija board. The *Scholar Goose* is the principal print voice of this brand of literary analysis, and from a recent issue of *TSG* a Planchet Defoliationist observes, "Anthropophagi are more numerous in our history and literature than the layman can imagine. The beheading, for example, of John the Baptist rings of more than the sadistic revenge of an exposed adulteress; for anthropologists, who presently desire anonymity, but who believe they have uncovered the prophet's remains, report that the skull is split open—an indication that the brains were cannibalized. Consumption of body parts—especially lips, ears, eyes, and gray matter—has always been considered a way to gain control over the soul of the one slain."

Wow. It is absolute and total vengeance, I'd say, whether you know it or not. And it might be good for you in other ways.

Anthropophagus is from the Latin, *anthrōpophagus,* and the Greek, *anthrōpophagos.* It is a synonym for cannibal, of course, which is from the Spanish, *Canibalis,* and the name that Christopher Columbus gave to those man-eating natives of Cuba and Haiti, the Caribs. Sometimes etymology is the proverbial snap, you see.

So to return to the course of the opening premise, eating human flesh, while deplored by a supposed unanimity of modern *Homo sapiens,* occupies a more fascinating and unexplainable niche in human evolution and propagation than you think. No single explanation for cannibalism's prevalence can be agreed upon by anthropologists and literary critics, but more evidence of its currency—latent and blatant—falls out of the closet or rolls out of the tool shed every month. This month it is T. S. Eliot, according to Veronica Grendel, a graduate student at the University of North Carolina, Chapel Hill, in the new paranormal literary criticism program there. Ms. Grendel's recent article in the *Scholar Goose* (from which the passage quoted above comes) goes on to suggest that Mr. Eliot may have been introduced to the joys of cannibalism by a young French medical student, one Jean Verdenal, who shared a Paris residence and a relish for symbolist poet Jules Laforgue with T.S.E. in 1910 and early 1911, about the time Eliot completed "The Love Song of J. Alfred Prufrock," wherein flounder the lines, "Though I have seen my head [grown slightly bald] brought in upon a platter, / I am no prophet." It is, according to Grendel, a double allusion but one that Eliot considered deleting from the poem until Verdenal showed him an 1896 drawing by Belgian impressionist James Ensor entitled *The Dangerous Cooks.* The work is one of Ensor's most famous satires. Explained simply, it depicts an Ensor colleague dressed as a chef, serving the head of the artist to a table of hungry critics (then living and recognizable) seated in the back room of a restaurant, where they revel and vomit in anticipation of seeing the heads of other painters (also then living and recognizable) being likewise prepared and garnished in the drawing's foreground. Art historian Susan M. Canning adds, "By placing his head on a platter like John the Baptist, Ensor envisions himself as a martyr for modern art and his own spiritual cause. Drawing on the image of *Modernity,* an 1883 etching by fellow Vingtiste Félicien Rops, in which a woman carries the head of an academic painter on a platter, Ensor represents his belief in his own centrality to Belgian modernism alongside the foolish behavior of his contemporaries who have failed to recognize his importance and his sacrifice."

Shades of Prufrock's problems, is it not?

But how do we know Eliot knew the Ensor drawing, later a painting? Well, the likelihood is twofold, says Veronica Grendel. Her computer informs her that Ensor was featured in an 1896 issue of the Paris art mag *La Plume,* and her Ouija board notes that some Ensor could have hung in a Paris Gallery in 1910–1911. Verdenal and Eliot were gallery regulars around Paris, and the Frenchman owned back issues of *La Plume*, according to answers to international inquiry in Grendel's e-mail. So why not? And when Veronica Grendel, or some other hungry Planchet Defoliationist, learns about exhibition catalogs, catalogues raisonnés, and some of the other handy tools of art research and scholarship (books, for instance), the maybes in the bio might dissolve.

As for the specter of cannibalism (good grief, another c-word), Grendel claims that French med school records show that one J. Verdenal was placed on probation in 1910 on suspicion of cannibalizing fresh cadavers, an atrocity of which he was supposedly cleared, the testimony of an American poet being key to the student's acquittal. "Combine this juicy ramification with certain psychological readings of *The Waste Land* as a disturbed and personal epic of guilt over homosexual passion and consequent repulsion by heterosexual sexuality (specifically here Tom's well-documented ordeals with his unfortunate first wife), and you have a picture of the young T. S. Eliot that is awfully modern still," Ms. Grendel writes, "yet so deliciously post-pagan that it is no surprise that the basically puritanical Mr. Eliot soon rushed into the forgiving arms of the Church of England following his Paris carousings."

In a nutshell, then, Veronica Grendel's paranormal lit crit says that during his foggy Paris year or so T. S. Eliot partook of cannibalism and homosexuality or at least thought about it. Via PC mouse and Ouija planchet, Ms. Grendel has pasted up a collage that, if not convincing or credible, is nevertheless occasionally charming and incredible. Just picture such a critic alternating between computer screen and voodoo particle board to fill out those mysterious voids in literary history and such. Or to frame the methodology with a more accessible and traditional analogy—if you can't find it in the library, ask your magic eight ball.

Enough.

Already I envision yards of grimace above the various chins of my editors, and readers perhaps. And I hear a voice: "My god, Schrapnel, why do you give ink to literary loonies like Veronica Grendel, William F. Scarlet, et al.? Isn't literary criticism already rocking in straits too perilous for words?"

I guess so. But what do you truly want here? Jacques Derrida? Frederick Crews? Some vintage Cleanth Brooks? Oh, gag me with a CD-ROM! My instinct declares that so many people of the business of books, literature, teaching, and up-market journalism like to see the aesthetic salad tossed with a Swiss Army knife once in a while. T. S. Eliot is a great poet no matter what he ate or with whom he slept. I may be wrong, but . . . well, you know.

Be careful, Schrapnel. You ought to know that the last time someone published something perverse about T. S. Eliot (John Peter's 1952 interpretation of *The Waste Land* as, among other things, a deeply personal, autobiographical poem that wrestles with sex hatred and homosexual passion) solicitors, acting on orders from T.S.E., confiscated copies of the magazine and removed the article or destroyed the journal. Furthermore, Eliot, via his thugs, sent a note to Mr. Peter expressing his outrage and disgust and demanding that the author keep his Freudian crap in check or else. Peter backed down, of course, but a few years after Eliot's death he wrote a postscript for a reprint of the censored essay, wherein he recounts the scenario with Eliot and his thugs. One wonders, based on Eliot's wild and uncharacteristic response to Peter's analysis, if a very raw and true nerve was not struck. But don't you just love what those young graduate students can do with a little technology, a few screwball lectures, and parapsychology apparatus?

Martin W. Ellison, Ph.D. ret.

Harvard, Mufton, Slippery Rock

Veronica Grendel has mysteriously withdrawn from classes this semester. She is but six hours of course work and one defense away from her doctorate. Friends and professors know not where she's gone. Stuffy-looking men in three-piece suits were seen entering her apartment complex a week prior to her disappearance. You could be next. But where will you go?

Anonymous
North Carolina

No doubt a premier lacuna in T. S. Eliot scholarship is the nature of his relationship with Jean Verdenal, who perished in 1915 in the Dardanelles as a member of the medical corps. The fact that Eliot dedicated his first volume of verse to Verdenal, and not to a family member, or his first wife, or Ezra Pound (the man solely responsible for Eliot's early success and recognition), is more than a mere oddity. But since T.S.E. sealed his personal notes from biographers, a felonious effort may be necessary to uncover the sleaze that a few critics suspect. Valerie Eliot claims that none of her husband's letters to Verdenal have survived, yet several Verdenal-to-Tom missives appear in her edition of the Eliot letters. Verdenal obviously harbored a strange and powerful affection for T. S. Eliot, the basis of which is not clear or obvious. I suspect that documents are yet suppressed. T.S.E. despised biographers and was more of a critical Formalist than he let on. Formalism, that close and boring textual study, is the fashionable and necessary critical retreat and preference endorsed by the writer who perhaps has much to hide.

Anonymous
Key West, Fla.

Holy tiger testicles! The image of T. S. Eliot eating human flesh with a homosexual lover or whatever . . . you ought to be writing for the *Scholar Goose* as well. Is it any wonder that professors of English and their kind are quickly moving up the ladder of NO CONFIDENCE to that rung presently occupied by lawyers and TV talk show hosts?

Mabel W. Stein
Santa Fe, N.M.

It was an 1898 issue of *La Plume* that featured Ensor and Rops. Ensor's first major Paris exhibition was in 1928, and by then Eliot was the affectatious snob we all know him to have been. The above facts can be found in books. The suggested connection between Eliot's allusion and the Ensor painting does not appear to be stable, something like your own critical methodology and that of the UNC grad student. Furthermore, Ouija boards and eight balls have been standard clandestine equipment in art criticism for over a century. And if there is any truth in that primitive logic behind cannibalism, that one acquires the traits of the one eaten, I pray that you, upon the occasion of your death, will be immediately cremated. Don't take it personally, for I do sometimes enjoy what I think is your satire. But I have known students in both the English and journalism major who would take you for fact and gospel. And that is partly why I took early retirement from the university. I am not for censoring what you write, but if you have anything that resembles a fan club, I support humane methods to exterminate it.

Ross Von Meterboro
Paris

SAVE THE WORDS: SCHRAPNEL'S LIST 2

Last summer, in the swift-hitting literary magazines that sport this column, began my list (or annual six-pack) of words that concerned and zealous language buffs ought to indulge in print and voice more often; thus a call to save said words from the cold fates of disuse and anachronism. Here goes again, in no special order of matter.

1. *Goon* is a good word. As a noun it is always (almost) pejorative and circulates in two senses. There is *goon*—a stupid person—from *gony,* a sixteenth-century synonym of simpleton, booby, or flaming rectum. American college students of the late 1930s popularized *goon* in this sense, as in "Martin, when he wears that Ezra Pound mask and swings his hairy arms and drools, looks like such a goon."

From the Hindi word *gunda*—a hired ruffian; enforcer—comes the second kind of goon. In last month's issue of *Radical Green Machine* an account of corporate goonery in the Pacific Northwest blames lumber company money for the rout of Earth First! protesters: "Ten thick, tall goons beat up a dozen women and children, smashed their dulcimers and flattened tires on their Volkswagen buses." Something like that. But of course there is the brighter side of goonery, as with professional hockey's New York Rangers and their acquisition of the 1994 Stanley Cup.

Goon is lately a verb too, like this: "Don't goon the professor while he's at the water fountain." Or to resort to NHL history once more, "Adam Graves goons Lemieux, breaking his hand and giving the Rangers the edge in the playoff series." Not.

2. Many readers and writers wax weary of cliché sentences like "—— is an oasis for ——," though legions still spout, scribble,

and keystroke them. But oasis is an old and refreshing phenomenon that, if sought and encountered in moderation, rejuvenates on myriad levels. In sound and association oasis is an aesthetic pleasure as well. Oasis promotes visions of a positive nature, connotations that encompass quenching and camaraderie, unless the water hole is surrounded by Huns. An apparently appalled camera man recently dismissed by the network that carries the Rush Limbaugh Show, however, was heard to refer to the studio in which the program is shot (so to speak) as "the asshole oasis." And this unfortunate usage of oasis should not have been printed, verity or not.

3. If something is *surreal* it is "characterized by fantastic imagery and incongruous juxtaposition of subject matter" (*The American Heritage Dictionary*). And while surreal and surrealism are terms overused in the arts and literature communities, so what? What else is there? Realism? Reality? Get real! Civilization has been evolving toward the surreal norm since the discovery of fire. All that is deemed outstanding in a given historical epoch is so because of its surreal ambiance. Witness now the appearance of Richard Nixon on a postage stamp, the ghost of Northrop Frye on *Saturday Night Live,* and that insipid TV adaptation of Dickens's *Hard Times.* (Now, I know that my readers are well educated and that the inclusion of the name of the author of *Hard Times* should insult most, because they know what it is. But I am not in control of where this piece may fall, where copies will wind up, and ergo who requires additional facts. As for Northrop Frye . . . hell, I just cannot do it all, even though I can include random internal rhyme, at times, in the parenthetical zeal, so surreal, as the banana peel.)

Nevertheless there is confusion and debate about the origin of the word *surreal,* from *surrealism.* Many lexicographers, etymologists, and Europeans credit avant-garde guru Guillaume Apollinaire (Wilhelm Apollinaris de Kostrowitzky) with the coinage, which first appeared in print about one year before his death in 1918. On the label of a bottle of moonshine, however, that is the centerpiece of the Museum of Appalachiana, in Princeton, West Virginia, you can read the following: "Sireel spirits, don't drink the hole thang ir yule draw weird pitchers on the outhouse wall!" The whiskey was bottled in 1886, the summer that Mark Twain visited Princeton and was arrested for vandalizing a local barn by painting "your whiskey is evil" on the building's west side, in white letters three feet high. Local lore also includes tales of Twain's escapades with certain harlots brought in by train from Charleston and a week of carousing that rivals even today's pulp fictions, prime time TV, and political conventions.

4. That laughing, onetime introductory chant to the old rock instrumental "Wipe-Out" echoes through pop music history like those airplane tragedies that took down the likes of Richie Valens, Jim Croce, and Stevie Ray Vaughn. *Wipeout* is a noun in surfer jargon to denote a violently failed ride, a dumping. And as a verb, *wipe out* means about the same, you see. So if something is a wipeout, it is a floundering failure, as in the now nonexistent environmental platform of the Clinton administration, which now makes the Republican assault on endangered species and the general beauty of the American landscape a proverbial cakewalk. In addition, if one is wiped out, he/she is verily exhausted or chemically altered. Maybe both. If one has an aversion for things spawned in the sixties, one may avoid the word. As for the hyphens between *wipe* and *out,* current style most often drops them. Ask any environmentalist for suggestions as to where you might stick them.

5. You don't hear the verb *skunk* much anymore, as in "Too many conservatives sure do skunk up the place" or that redundant headline "Giants Skunk Knicks, 189–0 in Meadowlands Benefit." Also, the common skunk (*Mephitis mephitis*) as roadkill on American highways is a rarer sight every year, like so many other four-legged mammals being suffocated by the ooze of *Homo sapiens* about the continent as you read. And while you cannot save the skunk from extinction either, you can still say it.

6. Although *therefore* and *ergo* are two-syllable synonyms, *therefore* is more often used. *Ergo* should be commoner because it has fewer letters. Brevity counts.

There you have it, word wranglers!

Once again a contest as to who can write the best sestina, employing Schrapnel's List 2 as the end words, is sponsored by participating literary magazines in "Adventures in Etymology." Last year's winner was Maureen Welsh-Mahoning from San Francisco. The poem (though a first-placer) was so bad, however, that none of my editors chose to publish it; but I am still trying to persuade them. Today's problem is that so far I have no "participating magazines" on the contest end of the column. Also, the MLA has pulled out of the prize pool, so there will be no *MLA Handbook for Writers* awarded to second place and no free back issue of *PMLA* for third. The times are tight. Nor does it help that over the past months my Adventures have riled or offended hundreds of colleagues supposedly in those good old high places. So I may be wrong; but I doubt it.

This latest list of yours is a real skunk itself. Sounds like you run out of ideas each summer and cough up some word phlegm and call it Schrapnel's List. Why don't you just take a vacation, as William Safire does, and let some more qualified and interesting etymologist take over? Go visit Bosnia, and don't wear a helmet.

Unsigned
D.C. postmark

Indeed I can think of no writing venue where brevity is more necessary and welcome than your Adventures in Etymology. If stagnation . . .

William P. Sound
Lobster Claw, Newfoundland

What I wanna complain about is General Motors and Lincoln makers. Every year they must make thousands of Cadillacs and Continentals where the turn signals don't work, and instead of fixing them or recalling them they just send them to their dealers in Florida to sell to some old retired bastard who just drives around twenty miles under the speed limit and you never know what the hell their gonna do.

Harry Capers
Tampa, Fla.

As far as I know, that green maniac acquaintance of yours, Mr. Forrest Jones, has yet to goon Ted Nugent. Did Jones wipe out on some surreal campaign against the purported corporate skunks who continue to rape oasis earth? I suspect not. Ergo, Jones is still at large, and the continued publication of your column is proof that nonsense counts for something also.

Regina Bovary
Bottleneck Grove, Ind.

Blast these lists of yours, Schrapnel! As you once wrote, "Words will be words." You make a good case for some words, but overall you have to realize that you pen a lame lament. Let language run its natural course, and if the original meaning of a word comes back to you, then you know it was meant to be. If not, call it fate, progress, illiteracy . . . whatever works. And realize that unless genetics holds more potential than we presently know (cf. *Jurassic Park*), we will never see a live dodo bird. And whether you're wrong or not, shout it! In my therapy groups we may traumatize a lot of eardrums, but we smile a lot too.

C. F. "Smiley" Day
The Institute of Sun & Games
Reno, NV

Surreal, to denote your usual mind-set, smacks as obvious as scum on a summer pond. And in that great pond of the literary life, you are the fattest and slowest carp. Get a job.

Melvin Wilson
Poetry Corner, Colo.

MANIFEST GREENERY

Green, that color in the spectrum between yellow and blue, the hue of growing grass and maturing leaves . . . green is getting grendelish. *Green* is from Old English and is formed from the same prehistoric Germanic base that produced the verb *grow, grō.* Green today refers to people who support conservation, ecology, environmentalism. In this sense it is a translation of the German, *grün,* and a lexicographic spinoff from the name of the West German political lobby of the early seventies, Grüne Aktion Zukunft. One popular English dictionary defines *green* in this context as, "a supporter of a social and political movement that espouses global environmental protection, bioregionalism, social responsibility and nonviolence." To the "nonviolence" component of the definition I can say swine bath, because some greenies are getting grendelish. *Grendelish,* a Schrapnelism from *Beowulf,* means monstrously dangerous, fiendish, marauding, homicidal. Behold.

A fortnight ago I received in the mail a large, dirty envelope, nine by twelve, postmarked São Paulo, Brazil. Ponderous were the contents of the package, containing clippings from American newspapers, bad and ghoulish photography, leaves of dried grass, a cardboard coaster from the Cork Street Tavern, six yards of monofilament fishing line, a thirty-five-page manuscript entitled "Deep Green Manifesto" (some of which was highlighted in green), and a forceful cover letter. To summarize, the people who sent this material demand that I and my editors publish highlighted excerpts of the manifesto, which in part read like the rant of an alcoholic, rattled Marxist and maybe an Edward Abbey impersonator following the wrong mushrooms. But after perusal of the enclosed clippings we got the big green picture. The writers of

DGM are radical (to say the least) environmentalists, already responsible for the death of over a thousand head of cattle in the southeastern United States. They killed the cows with canisters of nerve gas delivered in small homemade rockets. The reason for the slaughter was to force cattle ranchers from land next to wilderness areas where a reintroduction of red wolves and/or cougars has been proposed. The ranchers are trying to block this environmentalist project and have threatened to shoot, poison, or whatever any endangered species they deem harmful that may be released near their land. Cougars and wolves, the cattlemen say, could kill their cows, women, and children. Furthermore, the presence of an endangered species on public land makes purchase of the land for private enterprise nearly impossible. Meanwhile, the loss of several hundred head of livestock has already forced two ranchers to sell their farms to the Nature Conservancy and move to Miami Beach.

Authors of *DGM,* then, threaten to "terminate additional numbers of cows, chickens, and pigs, and whatever else we feel necessary, to curtail further rape of our beloved American wilderness or that is aimed at stopping the replenishment of wild land" [*sic, sic, sic*] unless their selected excerpts from their manifesto are published promptly. Realizing that these green nuts are serious, and technologically very sophisticated, and that even literary magazines must shoulder some moral responsibilities in this runaway age of Windows Whackos, my publishers and I (after days of soul-searching, conference calls, and packs of Tums) are caving in to the demands of these ecoterrorists. For the Deep Greens have promised to halt their deadly attacks if we run their critique of industrial society and humanity as a whole. By doing so, we believe we are preventing the senseless slaughter of many creatures, although the manifesto may set back the image of literary magazines and good writing by several generations.

Finally, it must occur to regular Adventures readers that the notorious Forrest Jones is behind the "Deep Green Manifesto." But I suspect he is not. For while much of the radical stance of the document is in line with Jones's ecoterrorist beliefs, the style of the articles bears not the charm, logic, eloquence, and literacy of Forrest Jones. The last rumor of his underground campaigns has him in Asia undergoing extensive cosmetic surgery. And of course, I know not how to contact him; nor would I if I knew. Nor will I recognize him, I am told, when or if I see him again. But I do hope that in those periodicals that carry second serial rights to this column, and therefore publish letters that the first runs spawn, a thorough reading of the mail will uncover a Forrest Jones missive. I know he is out there. I know he reads this; but goddamned if I know how he gets his copies or if he pays the full cover price.

From "Deep Green Manifesto"
    article one. mother earth is all ... mother earth provides for me and us ... therefore we cannot compromise where mother earth is concerned. ... protection of mother earth is the prime directive. ... we are willing and eager to die if necessary for our mother. ... it means we can kill for her too. ... the only true philosophy is the one by the deep greens. ... other enviromentals are weak and wavering while the industrial society eats away at mother. ... the continued development of technology will worsen the situation. ... it will certainly subject human beings to greater indignities and inflict greater damage on the natural world. ... things must stop.
    article seven. humanity is a demonstrated pestilence upon mother earth. ... so many human beings are driven by greed, lust and self-importance. ... therefore so many human beings are expendable. ... we are serious.
    article eight. we therefore advocate a revolution against the industrial system and the further spread of human population. ... this revolution may or may not make use of violence. ... it may be sudden or it may be a relatively gradual process spanning a few decades. ... we can't predict anything ... , but we do outline in some ways the measures that those who hate the industrial revolution and antienvironmentalism should take to prepare for a revolution against that form of society. ... sterilize almost everyone for at least forty years.

article thirteen. there are acceptable forms of violence that we endorse when extreme measures are necessary: assassination of politicians, business executives, and antienvironment people; extermination of livestock; termination of large and ignorant populations that infringe on sensitive ecosystems; elimination of anything that interferes with mother nature; flogging of those who pollute.

article seventeen. e.e. cummings is god.

article twenty-one. authors of this manifesto and officers of deep green are exempt from the declarations of article thirteen even in the event of a mistake.

article twenty-two. a roaring motorcar, which looks as though it were running on shrapnel, is the ugliest thing in the world and should be smashed along with personal computers, trail bikes, and snowmobiles. . . . furthermore, the book called ecodefense must be updated quarterly and distributed freely. . . . we advocate the monkey-wrenching and total destruction of construction heavy equipment all the way down to real estate agents and people who sell pesticides and herbicides.

article twenty-five. nature poetry must be taught in open air schools to our children and television must go, except the discovery channel. . . . natural food markets should be on every corner and at every crossroads. . . . fluoride is bad.

article twenty-nine. destroy all roads. . . . they are only there to scar mother earth. . . . destroy conformity and the aimless leisure class that democracy has spawned. . . . modern society cannot be improved and must be destroyed in order that we can return to the pristine state of wild nature and the beauty of mother earth. . . . close and destroy all golfcourses.

article thirty. everyone should pursue meaningful work or else. . . . artistic creation, social activism, and saving money are mostly meaningless activities, but at least they keep a lot of people away from the woods. . . . therefore we advocate self-reliance and civil disobedience, as well as a boycott of fast-food chains. . . . manual tools should be cleaned monthly and lightly oiled with a biodegradable lubricant.

article thirty-nine. early to bed and early to rise is not good enough . . . , because the god (or goddess) that holds you over the pit of hell, much as one holds a spider or some loathsome federal agent over a fire, abhors you and is dreadfully provoked. . . . deep green is not impressed either, but anonymous donations left behind designated boulders might help.

article fifty. society should make a concentrated effort to do without libraries, academies, fraternal organizations, organized religions, motorized things, letterman, pet rocks, and certs with retsin. . . . moby-dick is the best read for the real symbolism of the natural world and what is wrong with america.

here ends deep green manifesto and we trust you will think about it.

On behalf of our entire industry, I thank you for cooperating with the radicals in order to prevent further slaughter of livestock and perhaps the loss of innocent lives. We all know why God put us here, but it is a shame that there are small groups of radicals who want to ruin it for all of us. I am pleased to announce that since you printed the "Deep Green Manifesto" not a cow or pig has been mysteriously killed in our region, and our stock has risen five points on the New York exchange. While maybe some will greatly disapprove of your decision on this matter, we think you did the right thing. God bless you.

Samuel Jackson Barleycorn, VP
Bubba-Juke Steakhouses, Inc.

Why do you ignore the blatant plagiarisms in the "Deep Green Manifesto"? It contains thievery from a variety of dim-witted sources: Jonathan Edwards (the Puritan divine) to that looney Unabomber to a song I once heard sung by the Nitty Gritty Dirt Band. Certainly a closer scrutiny of the work will reveal even more plagiarism. But most of all, your giving in to terrorists' requests is a spineless act of fifth-rate journalism. Americans cannot bend to the wishes of cold-blooded murderers. This represents a nadir in the history of our publishing industry that I want all to know about. So if you don't publish my letter, I will key all of your cars.

Joseph Palmetti
Washington, D.C.

i mean, yo—schrap and company, what genitals—hey, if the deep greenies ain't bloody reds then i ain't the bite from the v—but you gotta know they read some books or two, wasted a moo or two, and yo, they groove on low e—the blue jeaned ape might be next—it's freaky, ladies and germs—but I love it—they can come flatten my pad any day—i'm for 'em—i'm turnin green—i'm on you!

frostbite freddy
the village

You can bet your best fountain pen, your latest version of Windows, the ranch, the kids, that Deep Green rules! You careless, degenerate, pig-breath morons—you greedy, thankless vermin that make up 90.0 percent of the human race! There's nowhere to run like the lemmings you ought to be. Gaia is the word. Apocalypse, yes! Most of you deserve it.

Dances with Elvis
Moose Runner Arrowsmith
Laureen Yellow Sky
Little Bird on Camp Stove
Bubbles on Sandbar
Grizzly Fumes—
"The Sioux City Six"

Art historians will notice that the "Deep Green Manifesto" contains references to, and plagiarisms from, a manifesto of Futurism by Italian poet and propagandist Filippo Tommaso Marinetti. Specifically, article 22's "roaring motor car, which looks as though running on shrapnel," is a poorly translated plagiarism taken largely out of context. Marinetti's contempt for libraries and the academy is also echoed by the Deep Greens. It disturbs me that people like that can get their dangerous, radical, and ill-educated views published through threats; but what is also upsetting is the misuse of ideas from an already deranged and outdated manifesto. To atone for this publishing blunder, I suggest you and your syndication friends donate ten thousand dollars to my library so I can buy more books.

Linda R. McKee, Library Director
The John and Mable Ringling Museum of Art
Sarasota, Fla.

It is disgraceful. You cannot trust killers, and I do not believe that publication of the "Deep Green Manifesto" will stop, or even slow, the enigma known as the green movement. What is also disturbing to me is the content and quality of the manifesto. There is nothing original in it. If the Deep Greens ever have an original thought, I expect it to despair and die of loneliness and isolation. What you have there is a lot of warmed-over Thomas Malthus, Thorstein Veblen, a dash of Marx, and a heaping helping of Dave Foreman in his youth, with a dessert from any TV evangelist clone. But ultimately, what we have here is a failure to communicate.

Burgess C. Woods
Birmingham, U.K. and Alabama

What a charming, yet unfortunately stupid, waste of ink and paper is the "Deep Green Manifesto." We have passed the point where anything significant can be done to slow, much less stop, the lumber of technology and the human swarm across the planet. Sex feels too good for most people to stop, and it doesn't take a genius or gynecologist to figure out what that thrill—multiplied by several billion times a day—means to the pipe dream called population control. Only a quick, violent, and mass extermination of 90 percent of humanity can save the planet now. Thus I turn my prayers and my giant transmitter to the stars in hope of attracting something like the Romulans or the Klingons who will cruise in here and clean house. It's that bad.

Beth Ogremason
Mt. Palomar, Calif.

At my camp in central Africa a copy of your column and the "Deep Green Manifesto" finds me. I am amused and marginally impressed. I know who they are, and I can tell you that their undergraduate GPAs were about a 3.2, or a low B. Two were chemistry majors, one is a graduate student in creative writing, and the other four were biology majors with areas of specializations ranging from ornithology to nuclear botany. These seven constitute the ruling body, the brains if you will, of Deep Green. Although the group has made some noise, my instinct says they are careless amateurs who will be arrested, probably next month when they try to assassinate that senator and that lumber company executive in Washington state. Philosophically though, I am somewhat at home with their enthusiastic contempt for the nonecology mind-set. Nor do I shun, as you know, assassination in time of war. More on this in a fortnight. Finally, your rumor mill is correct: you did not recognize me when I bumped into you last month at the Army-Navy Store in Mobile. Dr. Fang is a damn genius.

Forrest Jones
Go Figure??

FORREST JONES AND THE GREAT SASQUATCH COVERUP

Yes, another of those dirty nine by twelve clasp envelopes arrived at the P.O. box today. This one comes from Forrest Jones, the great green one himself, and the contents are verily shockful, stupendous, nearly unbelievable. If you yet think that the recent publishing blackmail called "Deep Green Manifesto" is gigantic environmental news, you are going to hyperventilate for hours after this Adventure. And by the way, the Deep Greens have so far kept their promise. No cows or related livestock have been nerve-gassed or otherwise exterminated since we printed their manifesto. So again, the critics and superfeds are wrong.

Now, as for Jones's latest, Forrest and company are unearthing a heinous ongoing plot of perhaps twenty years running perpetrated by the billion-dollar timber magnate Woodrow Wright and Sons. To be brief, the coverup involves some highly paid professional hunters, a few lumber company executives, and the supposedly mythical creature of the Pacific Northwest forests—Bigfoot. Let us quote here from Jones himself, for no one tells it like Forrest tells it: "We were camping in the deep, old growth forests of south central Washington when a cataclysmic thunderstorm nearly washed us off of the side of a verdant slope. Our business there was to monitor, and if necessary terminate, grizzly poachers who, it is rumored, sometimes brave this rugged and remote sector on behalf of oriental culinary interests. For six days we saw no signs of such scoundrels, although the presence of several old sets of ATV tracks perplexed us. Our always reliable counterintelligence in the Forest Service reports that this area had been closed to hiking and camping for many years but that some semiclandestine lumber company surveillance could have occurred. Virgin timber of course makes the logger mentality drool, ramble, and fondle uncontrollably. However, we found no dry slobber on flora or rocks.

"But after the aforementioned tremendous downpour, and thanks to a stench of unbelievable magnitude that lured us there, what we did discover was a large, shallow grave blasted open by lightning and washed out by the torrential rains. For nearly fifty yards down the mountain were scattered the skeletal remains and decomposing bodies of perhaps eleven very large primates. It seemed that six were females and five males, two males juvenile and one female, also preadult. Some of the skeletons were possibly six to eight years dead. The skulls of these creatures were in some cases twice the size of a human's head. All of the specimens had been shot several times with a high-powered rifle. The ribs and spines of several skeletons were chipped by bullets. Two decomposing bodies had gaping holes in their chests. The juvenile female had been shot twice through the head, and only half of the skull remained. One adult had six broken ribs from ballistical impacts.

"We spent two days restoring the grave site and selecting specimen parts for testing. We took seventy-two frames of photography. As we prepared to leave our incredible find, and were discussing the potential ramifications of the discovery, we were jumped by a man in camouflage clothing, pointing a large rifle at us. He was careless, however, in that he did not observe us long enough to know that we were a party of three and not two. Thus Clytemnestra, who had been off gathering huckleberries for the trek down the mountain, returned in time to disarm and disable the crudball before he might add us to the remodeled grave. This of course complicated our descent because we had to keep our attacker tranquillized for three days while we slipped carefully down the mountain and out of the thick old forest to our temporary headquarters.

"Once furtively and remotely encamped, we subjected the captured 'hunter' to hours of embarrassing torture. We extracted many details from him that I must condense severely here. Similarly, results of lab tests on the corpse and skeletal remains will be briefly related. But the forensics work was done secretly at a major anthropological research center also known for its expertise in DNA analysis. The scenario is this: for over fifteen years Woodrow Wright and Sons has been paying some highly skilled hunters to seek out and exterminate the remaining and very isolated populations of Sasquatch in the northwestern United States and neighboring regions of Canada. Yes, Bigfoot does exist! We have the bones and such (and the photographs) to prove it. We have the names of the principals in this ongoing plot, some confessions, and the names of hit men who also killed a few of the hunters that Woodrow Wright and Sons suspected might go to science or the tabloids for even bigger bucks, as in money, not deer. Also, we have confiscated a lumber company executive and his sparse records concerning Operation Squash Sasquatch, and we are prepared to turn over this prisoner, information, and documentation to reputable authorities, once we have been able to establish to our satisfaction which authorities are in fact reputable. Our various sources show that some knowledge of this genocide has been in the hands of the FBI, the CIA, and the Department of the Interior for over a decade. The Army Corps of Engineers may also be involved, and of course lumber companies in addition to Woodrow Wright and Sons have sweetened the monetary pot of this plot. Therefore details and information must be distributed with extreme caution, since too many heavy hitters seem to have paws in Operation Squash Sasquatch. There are many who would like to continue the murders and destroy the evidence. These are people dedicated to denying to the world the greatest anthropological discovery in recorded history. They represent, and will try to protect and promote, a billion-dollar industry whose sole activity is the butchering and leveling of America's old-growth forests, some of the scarcest and most beautiful remnants of raw, natural beauty left on this continent. These people are primarily mindless, greedy, soulless scums with little or no respect for life forms and interests outside of their own minuscule spheres of evil ignorance.

"Finally, what the presence of Bigfoot in North American forests means to science, ecology, and the insidious timber cartel is manifold almost beyond belief, as you can begin to guess. The communities of science and ecology must unite to shut down the lumber companies before they can destroy the remaining habitat of this magnificent, intelligent, and rare primate—a gentle, shy, and omnivorous being that our anthropologists believe is a cousin of Neanderthal man. Furthermore, those cretinous *Homo sapiens* responsible (directly or otherwise) for the slaughter of several dozen Sasquatch in the past twenty years must be imprisoned, drugged, and interrogated thoroughly.

"In short, that's our story, Schrapnel, my sometimes good man. And you are looking at the photos, I'm sure. Take it or leave it, as the vernacular jive goes. I think you will take it. Be on the lookout for more breaking news in the scientific journals soon. Also, you may want to watch your back now, whether you and your editors decide to publish this or not. This is the sort of news people will kill for, and some already have."

Indeed, there you have it, mythgoers.

I may not be quite a believer yet, but these are some terribly convincing photographs here, but too gory for a literary magazine or philological journal. So now the waiting ensues. And I wonder: is *Homo sapiens* ready for this, his long lost and secret cousin? Does it mean the kibosh for the timber industry? Will the obscenely wealthy nuts of the world hire great white (red, brown, yellow, or whatever) hunters to trash our temperate rain forests in an attempt to secure something rare and hairy for the den? And what about the "bring 'em back alive" guys that make their livings by zoo keeping and freak shows? Will the preachers want to get down on Darwin again? Will we forget the spotted owl? And most important, how will those purist readers of Adventures in Etymology respond to a column that entertains no etymologies??? For truly, is there a word that can contain or relate or describe this narrative from Forrest Jones?

To that last question I must answer a reverberating no! I may be wrong, but I doubt it.

Now that you have reduced your syndicate magazines to the level of supermarket tabloids, how about a catchy encore? Maybe you can have an extraterrestrial guest columnist next time, preferably some handsome Klingon? Or how about a little something on truffles by Howard Stern and Dr. Ruth? I'd like to read an explanation of El Niño by Stephen King that contrasts with Fidel Castro's views on the same phenomenon. Then close it out with a limerick by Rita Dove. Yes, sir, you've opened up some really endless possibilities now, you unliterary looney toon. Cancel my subscription.

Garrison Harrison
Garbles, Wash.

For several years now I have been turning to Adventures in Etymology for that unparalleled combination of wisdom and laughs that you always display and provoke. How fondly I recall such stimulating pieces, your columns on *bop, hood, romanticism, monster, poontang, literature.* How charming of you to coin *prufrockery* and *grendelish.* In addition, your readership is such an impressive and literate collage (for the most part), from university professors to park rangers to the chemically altered, to students, writers, teamsters, and housewives. You and your editors have, for so long, deserved nothing less than praise and applause for your motley yet germane contributions to American letters, to which the always riveting Cleopatra's Basket adds superbly. Thus it was with an otherworldly dismay, the likes of which I have not felt since my university English Department advertised in the *Chronicle of Higher Education* for three "remedialists," that I gasped through your latest Forrest Jones adventure, if you will. Now I ask you, have reality and aesthetics, language and literature, become so suddenly alien to your senses that you must stoop to relating an anthropological hoax to your usually sophisticated, or at least curious, readers? Bigfoot, Schrapnel?!? It is one thing to bemoan the emotional catastrophe of a friend and former colleague like Moe Hopswitch ("Monster Mash Revisited") but quite another genuine crock of piss to tell us, through the words of some freaky ecoterrorist, that Sasquatch exists. Well then, how about Yeti, Nessie, Elvis? Coming attractions, are they? I hope this recent abomination is not the harbinger of a sellout to the low Philistines of pop culture. Those of us who follow Adventures in Etymology for its insight and guffaws, its treks about our grand tongue and its literary artists . . . , we are sickened of late. Please, recover your errant soul, and no more Bigfoots.

H. Crawford Mizener, Ph. D., Ed.D.

Address omitted

In the summer of 1978, while camping near Mt. St. Helens, my wife and I saw a Sasquatch. Because such stories and their tellers have, however, for most intelligent people, all of the integrity and credibility of American professional sports, we chose to tell no one until now. It was a haunting few seconds that we recall as if it just happened at last year's Star Trek convention in Miami. The creature lumbered across a shallow stream a mere twenty yards from where we were rinsing our breakfast campware. The hairy ape stood up, probably six feet tall, on the far side of the brook, seemed to glare back at us for an instant, then hurried upright quickly and quietly into the dense forest. We crouched streamside for nearly an hour, speechless, motionless, and very uncomfortable. Then we arose simultaneously and bolted ten miles to the nearest dirt road. When we returned to the sight three years later, all of our camping equipment was gone, as was Mt. St. Helens. We hope this Forrest Jones and his friends can verify that Sasquatch does exist. But even if Bigfoot truly inhabits the old-growth forests of the Pacific Northwest, I wouldn't expect it or the endangered species lobby and faithful to be able to halt the gradual rape of the American wilderness by the timber industry. Environmentalists are often so naive. And scientists are mostly weenies. They often underestimate the widespread moral and ethical depravity of *Homo sapiens,* the general disconcern that the vast majority of humans have for things in nature other than themselves and the prime role of greed, money, and ego in human actions. Instead of raising romanticists like Thoreau, Carson, Brower, and Abbey to the level of guru, ecology buffs ought to have been reading the likes of Machiavelli, Napoleon, Rasputin, and Alexander the Great for foundations in philosophy and methodology. But it's too late now.

F. R. "Buddy" Olson
Monterey, Calif.

Oh, Schrapnel, you charlatan . . . you have at last wandered upon a topic about which you know even less than you pretend to know about language and literature—biology, I believe it is called. Or is it cryptozoology? In any event, my second cousin has some droppings he bought in Scotland last year that are probably those of the Loch Ness Monster. If you are interested, tough shit. He has promised them to Tipper Gore, who plans to surprise Al with them at their next Earth Day bash, whenever that lobby requires their attention again. Some gift, huh? As for you, I am beginning to wonder if *you* exist! I mean, can only one real person who is not certifiably schizophrenic beyond repair actually be responsible for Adventures in Etymology? I think this column is written by a committee of chimpanzees who loft marbles at a rubber keyboard that is connected to a Pentium computer. After spell check and grammar check, what comes out is Adventures in Etymology and an occasional sci-fi novel. I may be wrong but not as wrong as you.

Marcy Darcy-Lahoude
Perth, Australia

Don't you have a sweet job now? How do you get away with letting green weirdos and misanthropes write your columns for you? Your composition method resembles the tactics Tom Sawyer used to whitewash Aunt Polly's fence. Will we ever hear from B. M. W. Schrapnel again? In his own writ? And how will we know if we do? Or is this latest Forrest Jones hoax, preceded by that "Deep Green Manifesto," just your way of taking a vacation? Then again, do we want to hear from Dr. Schrapnel anymore? Or is this all some grand and despicable allegory that will need to be sorted out by the next generation of scholars and historians? Count me out.

Trudy L. Pasteur, Ph.D.
Oxford, Ohio

I can suggest numerous words for the Forrest Jones yarn. They are all so slanderous, repulsive, tasteless, and therefore unprintable, however, that I leave it up to you and your audience to think of them. Meanwhile, perhaps you should ponder where civilization would be without the materials to build fire, furniture, and the side panels of antique Ford station wagons, to say nothing of shelters from the storm. Any moron knows that trees can be planted and they will grow. As for Bigfoot, show me.

Marlin Woodson
Maryville, Mo.

 EXTRA! EXTRA!

Nearly all of us know the Indo-European and Latin roots of our word *extra*. Thus to spew the etymology here is pleonastic, nonessential, etc. Nor may it be relevant to where this essay goes today. Second, and for reasons not to be clarified for a paragraph or two, basic writing tutorage informs us that we should not rely on a thesaurus or synonym finder to spice our prose or verse without consulting a dictionary to verify the precision of the chosen synonym we want to employ in order to avoid repetitious diction. The observation, "Hawthorne's penchant for psychological ambiguity infuses his narratives with wide-ranging tension," for example means something very different from "Hawthorne's penchant for psychological ambivalence infuses his narratives with wide-ranging tension," even though *ambiguity* and *ambivalence* are suggested by those many reference books intended to help you expand and/or vary your vocabulary—well, those words are supposed to be synonymous. But if Hawthorne is ambiguous, he contains several levels or crannies of meaning. If ambivalent, he offers a simultaneous attraction toward and repulsion from an idea, theme, or symbol prevalent in his narrative. If Hawthorne is ambivalent he is undecidedly two-edged. When he is ambiguous, he is multileveled but not necessarily head to head in the grand arena of metaphor banging. It's confusing, I know. But it is also true.

So it was with something like ambivalence (to say nothing of chagrin) that I read in a rejection letter of my latest manuscript, by a university press, the following sentence: "I regret to inform you that the work is extralimital to the Press's current publishing goals."

Huh?

And next I asked myself, what in blazes does *extralimital* mean?

Well, I found *extralimital* in an unabridged Webster and not in *The Oxford English Dictionary.* Yes, I was surprised too. If something is extralimital, it is not found within a specified fauna area (as in extralimital species); or extralimital can mean "lying outside a specified part or surface; as in *extralimital* spots on a bird's wing." The word is an adjective employed in zoology. What the hell is it doing in my rejection slip?

Now, this particular university press editor—I'll call her Frank and not tell you the name of the publisher—well, perhaps she confuses etymology with entomology, as some readers of this column have done. Maybe she is trying to expand and popularize the usage of *extralimital* and daring to cross the borders of zoology. I do not object to coinage and fresh, variant applications. But isn't it disappointing enough to receive a publisher's decline in plain and simple language? Isn't it a tad cruel, sinister, and aloof to lace rejection slips with usage that is unusual and experimental? Or is it just me?

On the other hand, could it be that this university press editor commits the great thesaurus boo-boo, has caught—in her zeal to decline—a case of sick synonym syndrome (sss)? In any and either event, Dr. Schrapnel refuses to play multiple choice and tell you what he thinks happened, how he believes such a strange, and perhaps erroneous, employment of *extralimital* transpired, got there, and so on. After all, may there not be going on in Texas, er, I mean North Dakota, things with language that are boldly progressive and largely unknown? Then again, I could be fussing here over a typo; for *Webster's Unabridged* defines *extralimitary* as "being or lying outside the limit or boundary; as *extralimitary* land." Saying *extralimitary* is closer to formula phrases like "The book does not meet our current needs" or "While it seems like a worthwhile project, your proposal/manuscript does not seem to be right for our small list." And Webster contends in the second sense that *extralimitary* is "same as *extralimital*." Thus we go from geography back to zoology, and still no publishing bites on Adventures in Etymology—The Book.

Hell, yes, I am disappointed, I repeat. But I am not out of stamps or patience. And really, for pure charm and chutzpa you just cannot do better than those eight-and-one-half-by-eleven, take-this-book-and-shove-it (Professor) letters from the university presses. In addition, their letterheads are almost always very classy.

Again you spout common knowledge at your readers when you write that a thesaurus is a companion to a dictionary, I believe. I think you are telling your readers things they already know, in my opinion. And isn't it possible and advisable for writers on any level not to use a word in print that they can't use comfortably in speech. This is something that any writer worth his salt already knows. You don't need to remind us of something that everyone is aware of. The more I read you, the more I notice that you tell people about things that are well-known rules and concepts and give them information that is widespread and not so original. As a writer, one of the things about your job is that you are expected to come up with things that are fresh, like new ideas and observations. Things get real old real fast and they wear out. Unfortunately for you, you know you can't teach an old dog new tricks. So you should expect to be let go soon.

Marty M. Martindale
Martinsburg, W.Va.

I suspect that the editor who deemed your manuscript extralimital to the goals of her press was being kind and professional and was resisting descriptors like extraanal, extraasinine, extraneous, extramundane, or just plain lousy. But do not despair, Doctor. You yourself have declared in so many lunatic words than any idiot can get nearly anything published if he ascribes to a regular program of persistence, delusion, brown-nosing, and unprincipled harassment—or sends a postcard to a subsidy "publisher." I am roaring.

Marla Reed-Pikes
New York City

I cannot believe you have admitted rejection of your manuscript in your also worthless column. The news inspires me to throw a party and not invite you. It also tells us literate, educated readers that sanity still prevails in a few small corners of the publishing world. Now, if some sort of precaution can be instituted by the U.S. postal service—some kind of ban on selling stamps to crackpots—bookstores may again become safe and wholesome places. Eat some rancid oysters.

Elvis Peebles
SUNY, Duluth

yo, dontcha just wanna leer on editors till they shrivel. . . . I mean dam um anyhoo coz here in the v. I got dozens a no joes from the likes that doan like . . . remem yore cretin remarka while ago an by the hey that author who split showed up at my c-bar an I told him bout k-nop-off affirmative an heez out there in the fall he telz me . . . you are not so bad either . . . send clean water please

frostbite freddy
the village

 WISDOM AND CYNICISM

In that overlooked masterpiece by Edward Abbey, *The Fool's Progress; An Honest Novel*, protagonist philosophy graduate Henry Lightcap declares, during his dinner/job interview with Gibbsie (the federal park superintendent), "The important thing, I think . . . is to avoid succumbing to cynicism—to that weary resignation that passes, in the decadent West, for wisdom and wit." There is a rickety equation here:

Wisdom = Wit
Wit = Cynicism
Cynicism ≠ Wisdom

And there must be a more precise way to represent this formula mathematically, but my editors will not care. So there you have it.

Indeed, discriminations are in order, as too often today *cynicism* is taken to imply a propitious grasp of the verities but for no good reason. But wisdom, ah, you know. Wisdom is right or lasting insight. It is the understanding of what is true. *The Oxford English Dictionary* defines wisdom as the "capacity of judging rightly in matters relating to life and conduct; soundness of judgment in the choice of means and ends." *Folly*, the *OED* says, is the opposite of wisdom. And surely it is folly, according to Abbey's hero, to think that wisdom and cynicism are reciprocative. You'll see.

Now *wit*, while sometimes deemed synonymous with wisdom, more specifically denotes "the ability to perceive and express in an ingeniously humorous manner the relationship between seemingly incongruous or disparate things" (*The American Heritage Dictionary*). According to the *OED*, *wit* once referred to the faculty of thinking and reasoning in general, as in losing one's wit, or mind. Come to think of it, it still can. In the sixteenth century, wit took on the colors of humor and cleverness that still speckle its contemporary usage. So occasionally wit can squat alongside wisdom on the synonym line; but actual wit needs to be distinguished from, say, snide innuendo. Or as Dorothy Parker's witticism goes: "Wit has truth; wisecracking is simply calisthenics with words." And that delivers us to the c-word, of course.

Oh, cynicism! Now, there lies a specter of sorts. Cynicism denotes a scornful, bitterly mocking attitude or quality. And a cynic is one who believes all people are motivated by selfishness (cf. Freudianism). There is classical etymology here. For the Greek philosopher Diogenes founded the Cynic school, which stressed self-control and the pursuit of virtue. *Cynic* is from the Greek *kúōn,* for dog. Diogenes and his Cynics, because of the doglike sneers they uttered during critical discourse, were often called *kunikós,* or currish. *Curmudgeon,* with roots heretofore uncertain or muddled, no doubt derives from this Grecian term too, although most lexicographers decline to believe so. I may be wrong, but I doubt it.

Holman's *A Handbook to Literature* defines cynicism as "doubt of the generally accepted standards of the innate goodness of human action. . . . Any highly individualistic writer, scornful of accepted standards and ideals, can be called cynical." She might also be called nihilistic or iconoclastic, don't you think? But what is verily alarming here is the not-so-loose equation of cynicism with individualism, which in art is sometimes a foggy, praiseworthy trait. You know—those highly individualistic writers and such, so ahead of their times, badly misunderstood by peers and put down as hacks—those poor paranoiacs past and present who therefore set off for Europe, England, Asia, Africa, maybe—or if absolutely cool—to Mexico, Alaska, New Zealand, or New York. My my, yes, cynicism is good under some covers.

Then we have reference books like *The Cynic's Lexicon* (St. Martin's, 1984), which editor Jonathon Green dubs as an amoral but necessary dictionary of largely negative and destructive aphorisms, heaviest with snot from Ambrose Bierce and Oscar Wilde.

The *Detroit News* says, "No confirmed crab should be without this book, for it is a veritable mother lode of ripostes, mockery, scorn and true wit." For sure, *The Cynic's Lexicon* exudes streams of trashing and wisecracking that flood everything under the sun (cf. Ecclesiastes), but true wit it is not. Unabashed cynicism it is, sprouting from that deep and smelly spiritual abyss where wit cannot grow. Ask anyone.

Also, there is *Shakespeare's Insults* (MainSail, 1991), subtitled "Educating Your Wit." The obvious insistence here is that a knack for insult distinguishes one as witty or something. My second cousin the former stand-up comic, who idolized, imitated, and plagiarized (albeit poorly) Don Rickles—well, cousin has had his jaw broken enough times that even chocolate milk shakes are impossible for him to chew.

"Analyze, don't diogenize," a philosophy professor once instructed. "The acquisition of wisdom is never easy, but it is usually rewarding. Wisdom may not wear a smiley face each day, but behind the fashionably smug grin of cynicism grows a brain tumor." I still believe that to be one of the silliest things an academic has ever told me. But you know, that prof, who requires anonymity, was once the president of an Ivy League institution. Furthermore, the verbalization (*diogenize,* from Diogenes, and meaning to render cynical) is darn charming, whereas a diogenical outlook is not. You see?

Finally, when the temptations of cynicism knock at your spiritual gate, it is a bromide to recall Diogenes himself, the archetypal cynic who wandered nightly, with a lantern, the streets of ancient Athens, looking for an honest man. Diogenes, who showed his contempt for life's amenities by living in a tub. Diogenes, who was known to bark, urinate, and masturbate in public.

Any questions, class?

(Editorial Note: Since its print debut a fortnight ago in the Journal of Cultural Calamity, *"Wisdom and Cynicism" has spawned a hoard of missives that rivals all Adventures in Etymology but perhaps "Romanticism Now and Then." Here are some of the more volcanic and germane; and I*

thank those readers who did not take up pen, keyboard, and/or plastic explosive. — *B.M.W.S.)*

Who cares what the *OED* says? It is an outdated lexicographic brontosaurus, top-heavy with Victorian conservatism and WASP chauvinism. Maybe I sound cynical, but you think about it. Furthermore, the *OED* shortchanges women in its quotations. You'd think that only men ever had anything exemplary to say. I say dump that dictionary and go with *The American Heritage* or one of the new unabridged Websters.

Molly Blevens
Bean Gas Bend, Tex.

Bravo! I too grow impatient with cynicism masquerading as wisdom and getting away with it. To modify one of Hemingway's observations, nowadays one needs a built-in, shockproof crap detector to rise above the lazy "thinking" that passes in the streets, in the media, and in some scholarship as accurate analysis. True wisdom (or wit) is not (as they say) easy to come by. Harlots and cynics are. Our schools need to teach more logic and critical thinking. Screw those anything-and-everything-goes attitudes. And how about that genuine false dilemma being debated so seriously by your literature colleagues: Multiculturalism vs. The Canon? Diogenes, instead of looking for an honest man, should have devoted his carousing to the discovery of a wise one. Then again, would he have known? Or would he have stopped in front of the first mirror or fountain he encountered? Yes, classical anecdotes are so chockablock full of malarkey.

Winthrop J. Moss, Ph.D.
retired, living on the tundra

I guess you mean that "healthy cynicism" is an oxymoron. I've always been skeptical of my cynical uncle, the former university chemistry professor who now lives in a cabin on a remote hillside in Maine. He quit practicing chemistry and teaching because he said that some day chemists would find a way to reproduce everything and Nietzsche's myth of the eternal return would become a virtual reality nightmare, whatever that means. His colleagues always grinned at his "healthy cynicism" but secretly conspired, I believe, to give him the spiked punch at faculty parties, knowing full well he was a semireformed alcoholic.

Agnes Blundon
New York City

You, cynic of cynics and trasher of all things aesthetic and sound, have no right telling people what is wisdom and what isn't. How about this line from Shakespeare that I found in one of the books you maligned: "I find the ass in compound with the major part of your syllables." You think about it.

May B. Day
Martins Ferry, Ohio

Let us not overlook a horrid species of cynicism, certain television opinion/talk forums like that of Rush Limbaugh (as distinguished from those daytime freak shows of Donahue, Oprah, and their ilk). Limbaugh tries to pass off his halfbaked cynicism and political naivete as wisdom and wit. Your readers may be interested in this revealing story: a teenage prank to which Limbaugh confesses cherubically is his soldering closed the doors to his local high school one night, so as to prevent or delay its opening the next morning. It is a fitting metaphor, that act, for so much that is necessary for the acceptance of his zealously "conservative" viewpoints and mindless, sneering hysteria. That is, too many educated people get in the way because they are not so easy to fool; they may not be duped by his fallacious arguments, mangled information, and garnished lies. Education, then, is the enemy. In addition, Frieda M. Frigmellon, noted sociologist at Boston College and an eloquent critic of the television talk show mentality, points in alarm to what may be the most horrifying element in hours hosted by the likes of Limbaugh—the audiences: "whole riots of fools, faces brimming with interest and belief, reasonably dressed, normal-looking and probably carrying voter registration cards one and all. . . . If that is not sufficient melodrama to prompt so many to flock again to Canada, then there must be drugs in some of our drinking water (or in the glue of postage stamps), insidious mind-numbing chemicals. The only possible antidote is a university education, although even then there are no guarantees or warranties. I don't even trust Ayn Rand anymore." She may be wrong, but I don't think so.

Marc Hill
Bethlehem, Pa.

Interesting that you choose a quotation from Edward Abbey to begin your essay on wisdom and cynicism. Abbey, to me, is an overbearingly cynical writer and not much of a thinker. His blithering romanticism masquerading as environmentalism is another shortcoming of his "philosophy." And although his infamous *The Monkey Wrench Gang* is a sort of gospel to the radical toe of the green movement, *The Fool's Progress* is his finest work by far, one that he himself referred to as "the thick masterpiece." It was the last novel he published in his lifetime and one that shines with some calculated insight absent from most of his environmentalist rants, as your quotation reveals. Perhaps in his declining years Abbey saw the holes in his raison d'être. Pity he is not around now to patch them, that time ran out on him, as it did for Henry Lightcap.

L. W. "Moose" Cravens
Casper, Wyo.

The Diogenes crab is a species of West Indian hermit crab, and like all crabs it will eat garbage, dead and rotting animals, even itself. There lies here a metaphor that I misplaced during my third brandy tonight, if you catch my tidal drift. Hope you and your readers enjoy it.

Oliver Borden
Rapid City, S.D.

You infinite bore! Having read and criticized you for years, I am nonetheless astounded by your bombastic gall. Why would any intelligent reader believe that you know the differences between wisdom, wit, and cynicism? Anyone who trash talks poetry readings, Republicans, Romantics, karaoke, Robert James Waller, the National Hockey League, and multiculturalism, and the great American publishing industry (to name but a spoonful) is not wise or cynical. I'm not sure there is a word for you and your writing, but finding it, I suspect, is an etymological and lexicographic adventure with no end. Go suck on a water moccasin!

Elvis Peebles
SUNY, Duluth

In addition, so many cynical aphorisms commit the informal fallacy of ambiguity we call the *fallacy of composition,* or reasoning fallaciously from the properties of the parts of a whole to the whole itself. A mere collection of cobblestones, for instance, is neither a road nor a house; and an assemblage of cretinous brawlers does not necessarily qualify as an NFL franchise or a citizenry, even in Cleveland or Los Angeles. I wish more people knew this.

Weldon Schoolcraft
St. Thomas, V.I.

Since the parade of cynicism's synonyms reads like the smart aleck's roll call, I doubt that many sensitive and well-read people will confuse it with wisdom. But you are right to suspect that cautions are sometimes in order. In believing so, however, you affect a cynical outlook. Therefore, how seriously can one take the warning about cynical thought from a writer whose very motivation grows out of pessimism, skepticism, and an ego on overload? How about them Deconstruction apples? On the other hand, one of the sad side effects of this age of the information superhighway, it seems, is that the turnpike is cluttered with clunkers as well as reliable vehicles, and even that close look under the proverbial hood before you turn the key is but a partial precaution against spiritual and intellectual breakdown. You, Schrapnel, are no Mr. Goodwrench, but you are often a good read against all odds. How do you like those fractured metaphors?

W. W. "Frenchy" Marquette
New York, Paris, The Alamo

 INDEX

Grey, Zane, 35
Grosbeak, Mary J., 35
Grubb, Senator C. Q., 83;
    on President Clinton, 83

Hardy, Thomas, 43;
    of moustache, 90
Harlequin Romances, 84
Harrison, G. B., 12-13
Hawthorne, Nathaniel, 84;
    ambiguity and ambivalence, 165
Heebs, Wellington, 54
Hemingway, Ernest, 19, 33, 46;
    "Nick and the Carrot Stick," 19,
        45;
    crap detector, 172
Hermeneutics, 51
Hill, Marc, 174
Hitler, Adolph, 31
Holman/Harmon, 70;
    Handbook to Literature, A, 75, 129,
        170
Holyoke, Reginald C. T., 90
Homer, 23
Hopps, M. M., Ph.D., 65
Hopswitch, M. A., 111, 162
Hussein, Saddam, 12, 86

ICBM, 64
Irving, Washington, 23-25, 28-29
ISFUPP, 102, 105

Jarrell, Randall, 60
John and Mable Ringling Museum of
    Art, 154
John the Baptist, 136
Johnson, Samuel, 12
Jones, Forrest:
    account of Sasquatch coverup,
        157-60;
    behind DGM, 149;
    Dungavenhooter, 113;
    hoax, 164;

maligned, 146;
    on Romantics, 86;
    on Ted Nugent, 107-08;
    on weenie, 41;
    response to DGM, 155-56
Journal of Cultural Calamity, 171
Journal of Degenerate Aesthetics, 77
Joyce, James, 33; Finnegans Wake, 56;
    Ulysses, 98
Jurassic Park, 87, 96, 146

Kahounos, Christos, 131
Keats, John, 132-33;
    "Ode on a Grecian Urn," 132-33
Kelly Girls, 82
Kesey, Ken, 89
Kevorkian, Jack, 114
Keys, Richmond, 91-92;
    Old Hitler; or, The Shark, 91-92
Kimball, Roger, 32
King, Larry, 65
King, Stephen, 161
Knight, G. Wilson, 79
Kruty, Paul, 60
Kruty, Peter, 60

Laforgue, Jules, 137
L'Amour, Louis, 31, 35
La Plume, 138, 141
Lars the Lipless, 14
Law of Denotative Explosion, 130,
    132
Lawrence, Barbara, 33;
    "Four-Letter Words Can Hurt
        You," 33
Lawrence, D. H., 68, 102
Legree, Uriah, 22
Lemieux, Mario, 142
Limbaugh, Rush, 74, 99, 103, 108;
    on President Clinton, 73;
    teenage prank, 173-74.
    See also Rush Limbaugh Show
Lovejoy, A. O., 83, 87

Luanamoa, Lance, 50;
  Crumb Snatchers Beware, 50

Machiavelli, 31, 163
Mad magazine, 117, 133
Madonna, 88;
  Sex, 88
Mailer, Norman, 34
Malthus, Thomas, 32, 155
Marinetti, Filippo Tommaso, 154
Marius, R., 32
Mars, Toulouse, 49–62, 68, 101;
  "Acquainted with the Ramps," 69–70;
  Donald and May Mooning at the Bay, 50;
  Glee, Sissy, and Me, 50;
  "Letters to the Editor," 52–54;
  Me Squeeze-Box, Yes! 50;
  notebooks, 69;
  Rat Hole Serenade, 49–55;
  "Sturm und Drang de Levi en Carpe Diem Baby," 52;
  Wanda the Warp, 56–62
Martindale, Marty M., 167
Marvell, Andrew, 37;
  "To His Coy Mistress," 37
Marx, Karl, 155
Masters and Johnson, 74
Matisse, Henri, 79
McDougalhenny, Fergus, 35
McGuane, Thomas, 47
McKee, Linda R., 154
McKuen, Rod, 54
Milton, John, 79;
  Areopagitica, 31–32;
  Thus Spake Misanthropos, 31–32
Mr. Goodwrench, 176
MLA, 75, 98, 145
MLA documentation, 3, 4, 81
MLA Handbook for Writers, 145
Moby-Dick (Melville), 130, 152

Modern Philology, 131
Montgomery Ward Catalog, 109
Morris, William and Mary, 27
Morrison, Toni, 130
Multiculturalism, 31, 131, 175;
  vs. The Canon? 172
Murray, James A. H., 25

Napoleon, 163
Nash, Ogden, 60, 117
National Hockey League, 90, 175
National Review, 51
Nature Conservancy, 149
New Americanist, 66
New Wave Calvinism, 50
New York Rangers, 142;
  Graves, Adam, 142
New York Review of Books, 29
New York Times, 89
New Yorker, 77
Nietzsche, F., 173
Nitty Gritty Dirt Band, 153
Nixon, Richard, 143
North, Thomas, 2
Norton, W. W., 101
Norton anthologies, 23
Nugent, Ted, 107–10

Okrand, Marc, 60;
  Klingon Dictionary, The, 60
Olivier, Sir Laurence, 26
Olympus, 3
Operation Desert Storm, 12
Operation Squash Sasquatch, 159
O'Shames, P. U., 64;
  Silly Sayings from Billary and Hill, 64
Oversoul, 55
Oxford English Dictionary, The, 21, 25, 73, 97, 125, 128, 166, 169, 172

Palm Beach Post, 90
Paranormal Literary Criticism, 136